QUICK
CUISINE

QUICK
CUISINE

LEWIS ESSON
with HENRIETTA GREEN & MARIE-PIERRE MOINE

Collier Books
Macmillan Publishing Company
New York

Maxwell Macmillan International
New York   Oxford   Singapore   Sydney

DEDICATION

To Colin Clark and Colin MacIvor
for their inspiration
and to Ajit

Throughout the book, recipes are for four people
unless otherwise stated.

Editorial Direction: Lewis Esson Publishing
Design: Sue Storey
Photography: Patrice de Villiers
Illustrations: Lynne Robinson
Food for Photography: Jane Suthering
Styling: Penny Markham
Editorial Assistant: Penny David
Production: Sonya Sibbons

First published in 1991 by
Conran Octopus Limited, London

Collier Books
Macmillan Publishing Company
866 Third Avenue
New York, NY 10022

Macmillan Publishing Company is part of the Maxwell
Communication Group of Companies

Library of Congress Cataloging-in-Publication Data

Esson, Lewis
    Quick Cuisine / Lewis Esson, with Henrietta
Green & Marie-Pierre Moine. — 1st Collier Books ed.
        p. cm.
    Includes Index
    ISBN 0-02-065038-8
    1. Quick and easy cookery. I. Green, Henrietta.
II. Moine, Marie-Pierre. III. Title.
TX833.5.E77 1993   92-42946   CIP
641.5′55–dc20

Macmillan books are available at special discounts for
bulk purchases for sales promotions, premiums,
fund-raising, or educational use. For details, contact:

Special Sales Director
Macmillan Publishing Company
866 Third Avenue
New York, NY 10022

First Collier Books Edition 1993

10 9 8 7 6 5 4 3 2 1

Printed in Singapore

CONTENTS

INTRODUCTION

This is a book for food lovers in a hurry – people who enjoy cooking and eating at home, but who don't usually have much time to spend in the kitchen.

The secret of Quick Cuisine lies in turning lack of time into an advantage. As with chefs in fashionable restaurants who create great dishes in minutes, the skill is knowing exactly what can be achieved in the time. Slowly simmered delicate combinations are out – instead bold fresh flavors, natural textures, and exciting combinations are the order of the day.

Quick Cuisine's approach is based on using the best possible fresh produce available. Quality ingredients are a must – since there is no time to nurture or disguise them, they will have to give of their best immediately.

The equipment required is quite basic, as found in most domestic kitchens, so there is no need to assemble a special batterie de cuisine to cook from this book. However, a good food processor, an efficient broiler, a large heavy skillet, a sharp knife, and a sturdy pair of scissors are all essential.

Preparation and cooking techniques are simple, if not obvious! The Quick Cook has to be prepared to be bold and use his or her hands for shredding or tearing leaves or for patting seasonings into food, for instance; to use eyes and instincts to judge weights and measures, and to exercise simple common sense and basic initiative at all times.

This hand-on approach of Quick Cuisine is fun and unpretentious. If you have previously been put off by the long lists of ingredients and finicky methods of traditional cooking, Quick Cuisine will make a confident cook out of you in no time at all.

1

THE QUICK APPROACH

The secret of Quick Cuisine lies in a very simple three-fold approach: buying the right ingredients, using labor-saving equipment, and employing time-saving techniques.

As Quick Cuisine makes the most of the natural full flavors of food, the ingredients must be truly fresh and of the best quality. It also takes advantage of today's wide range of ready-prepared food, from trimmed and washed salad leaves to filleted fish and cut-up poultry: the extra cost is more than justified by the time saved.

Apart from the essential food processor, the equipment we use is neither extravagant nor complex. Simple utensils, such as graters, zesters, good knives and scissors, and versatile woks, make possible many of the speedy preparation and cooking techniques we use.

These techniques are simplicity itself, to ensure the greatest effect with the minimum of effort: from straightforward short-cuts, like tearing ingredients or snipping them with scissors straight into the pan, to the correct way to broil or sauté for speed and effectiveness.

BUYING the BEST INGREDIENTS

• Buy the freshest food you can find.

• Buy "little and often" – even items such as spices!

• Make the most of seasonal produce.

• Buy from reliable suppliers where freshness and quality are guaranteed.

• Where appropriate, make use of convenient packages of prepared food: boned and trimmed meat, skinned and filleted fish, washed, trimmed, and cut vegetables and salad leaves, and so on.

• Use fresh herbs for more potent flavors. Grow them in pots on the kitchen windowsill or stand cut bunches in water in a shady place. Cut herbs also keep well wrapped in damp newspaper inside a plastic bag in the refrigerator. Generally in this sort of speedy cooking, dried herbs don't have time to develop their full flavor.

• Use best quality extra-virgin olive oil for salad dressings and most cooking. A mixture of equal parts olive oil and sunflower oil can also be used for cooking; it has a less intrusive flavor which may sometimes be critical.

• Unsalted or low-salt butter allows you to adjust the seasoning yourself, especially in flavored butters with salty ingredients such as anchovies or cheese, and it is essential when making sweet butter sauces.

• Use the same wine in cooking as you drink – so-called "cooking wines" can ruin a dish.

• Use wine or cider vinegar rather than distilled or malt for a better, more subtle flavor.

• Use freshly ground black pepper for greater pungency.

• Use coarse salt as it brings out the flavor of food more powerfully and you'll need less – especially if you use a salt mill.

• Try to buy uncoated lemons and oranges if you are going to use the zest. If you can only get waxed fruit, scrub them thoroughly in hot soapy water, rinse well, and pat dry.

• TRY TO KEEP THE FOLLOWING STAPLES ON HAND:

loaf of good bread
head of garlic
package of coarse (sea) salt
package of black peppercorns

● ALWAYS HAVE THE FOLLOWING ESSENTIALS
IN THE REFRIGERATOR:

eggs
milk
unsalted butter
2 or 3 lemons
1 or 2 oranges (or some fresh orange juice)
bunch of scallions (green onions)
bottle of dry white wine
$\frac{1}{2}$ pound bacon
plain yogurt
heavy cream, or crème fraîche
$\frac{1}{4}$-pound chunk of Parmesan cheese
jar of good mustard, preferably Dijon
$\frac{1}{2}$ bottle dry sherry

● KEEP THE FOLLOWING FOR BACK-UP IN
THE FREEZER:

another loaf of good bread
package of English muffins
$\frac{1}{2}$ pound butter
leaf spinach
petite green peas
good vanilla ice cream
chicken stock
ice cubes

● STOCK YOUR PANTRY WITH THE FOLLOWING:

10-minute rice
dried pasta
easy-cook Chinese noodles
extra-virgin olive oil
sunflower oil
walnut oil
Chinese chili oil
red wine, white wine or cider vinegar
sherry vinegar
balsamic vinegar
soy sauce
mustard powder
five-spice powder
Worcestershire sauce
anchovy paste (keep in refrigerator once opened)
tomato paste (keep in refrigerator once opened)
Tabasco or other hot pepper sauce
harissa sauce or other hot pepper paste
whole nutmegs
paprika
cumin seeds
small dried chili peppers
sun-dried tomatoes in oil
capers
granulated sugar
brown sugar
confectioners' sugar
honey
red currant jelly
marmalade
blanched almonds
seedless raisins
pine nuts
walnuts
hazelnuts
poppy and sesame seeds

● KEEP THE FOLLOWING FOOD IN CANS:

clams in brine
tuna fish in oil
anchovy fillets in oil
artichoke hearts
cannellini beans
chick peas (garbanzos)
baby lima beans
whole-kernel corn
pimientos
crushed tomatoes

● A well-stocked liquor cabinet is an asset in this sort of cooking. Essentials include vermouth, rum, whiskey, brandy, and the black-currant cordial, crème de cassis. Hard cider is also very useful but, like sherry, should be kept in the refrigerator. Unlike wine, it is quite acceptable to cook with an inferior brand of spirits, such as brandy or rum, in order to save the better brands for drinking. Many liquor stores and supermarkets stock a wide range of miniatures of brandies and liqueurs which are very handy for cooking.

LABOR-SAVING KITCHEN EQUIPMENT

• Most quick cooking depends on a good food processor. If you don't already have one, buy one of the new designs with a detachable small bowl within the main bowl for chopping small amounts. Give the machine a permanent place out on the worktop so you don't have to lift it out of a cupboard each time you want to use it.

• Good chef's knives save time. Have at least 3 in different sizes, and sharpen them regularly. Also buy a small stainless-steel fruit knife with a serrated edge. Keep knives in a handy place so they are always within easy reach.

• Have a couple of good pairs of all-purpose kitchen scissors and keep them sharp. They are useful for everything from cutting up poultry to snipping herbs.

• A lemon zester lets you to pare off strips of peel from citrus fruit without taking the bitter pith underneath.

• Have several large, sturdy chopping boards. Keep one exclusively for preparing raw meats.

• A good pastry or paint brush is useful for applying oil to food, but avoid nylon bristles as they may melt on contact with hot food.

• A salad spinner gets leaves really dry and saves a lot of time otherwise spent patting them.

• A wok is essential for stir-frying. Get one with a matching scoop to stir the food with. The single-handled versions are easier to maneuver. Buy the very basic and inexpensive ones from Chinese grocers that can be replaced readily.

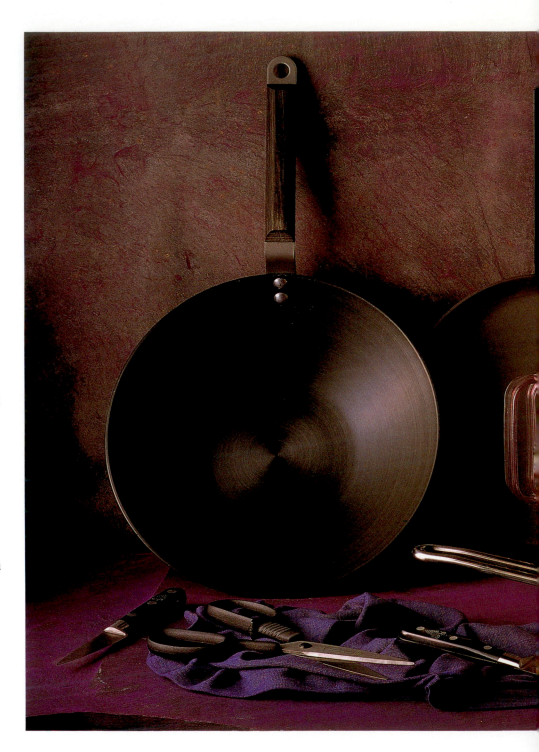

• A good quality sauté pan is worth the investment. Make sure the base is thick and heavy, for even browning, and that the sides are quite high, so that the food can be stirred vigorously and liquid ingredients added later. It should also come with a tight-fitting lid for subsequent slower cooking after the initial browning.

• A proper pasta pot, tall with an inner basket so that the pasta can be lifted from the water with ease, is expensive but it will pay for itself many times over.

• Try to have one or two skillets in different sizes, to match the type and quantity of food being cooked. Nonstick pans are best as they permit healthy dry-frying. A small omelette pan is also very useful.

TIME-SAVING TECHNIQUES

● Snip herbs and leaves with scissors directly into pans or salad bowls rather than chopping them on boards. Firm fruit and food such as chicken livers, mushrooms, and sliced cooked meats can also be snipped.

● Tear or shred food like salad leaves or cooked chicken into bowls or pans. This is not only quicker than chopping, but gives a better texture and keeps more of their juices.

● Wherever possible, crumble and flake foods like cheese and cooked fish into pans and bowls rather than taking the time to chop them.

● Many foods, including firmer vegetables as well as cheese, can be shredded instead of finely chopped. For larger quantities, do it in the food processor.

● Our phrase "whizz in the food processor" means processing just long enough to achieve the desired texture. It is usually necessary first to break the food into manageable pieces so the machine can deal with them efficiently. When whizzing, be careful not to over-process foods as they can easily become a textureless mush.

● Quick cuisine makes a great deal of use of the zest of citrus fruits. Use only uncoated or well scrubbed fruit. Grate the zest with the fine section of a grater or pare it with a zester. Either way, try not to press too hard so as not to take too much of the bitter pith underneath the peel.

● A quick and easy means of flavoring with garlic is to halve a clove and rub it over the bottom of a pan or bowl or even smear it directly over firm food. Otherwise, crush cloves with the side of a wide knife or use a garlic press.

● As Quick Cuisine does not really allow the time for marinating, we make much use of flavored pastes and crusts when broiling, pan-frying, or baking. The pastes are usually bound with oil to ensure that they stick to the food during cooking. Paint them on with a brush, spread them on with a spatula, or simply press them on with your hands.

● For those dishes that require boiling water, to speed things up heat the water in the microwave oven. For dishes like pasta, when you need a large amount of water, heat some in the microwave and the rest in the pan.

● Most meat needs to be seared in the early stages of cooking to seal in its juices and give it a good color. Don't be afraid of using high temperatures to achieve this as rapidly as possible.

● When broiling, heat the broiler as early as possible so that it has the time to get thoroughly hot while you are preparing the ingredients. Try to use only uniformly thin pieces of food for quick and even cooking.

• Sautéing is a very useful technique in Quick Cuisine. The main ingredients, usually cut in small pieces, are initially cooked in butter or oil, with frequent stirring, over high heat to brown and seal them. Flavorings, such as wine and herbs, are then added and the dish simmered gently for a few minutes to finish the cooking.

• Stir-frying is similar to sautéing, but is done in a wok. The food is again usually cut into strips or small pieces and is kept on the move all the time over quite high heat. The shape of the wok allows cooked food to be shoved to the cooler top of the rim while new ingredients are cooked in the hotter bottom.

• Liquids, especially sauces, are often reduced to intensify their flavors and thicken them to a required consistency. They are simply boiled rapidly for as long as is necessary. The wider the pan, the faster the liquid will evaporate, but if the pan is too wide it can be difficult to control the process.

• After food has been pan-fried or broiled, the pan is often deglazed with a little liquid, usually water, stock, vinegar, lemon juice, or wine or other alcohol. Stirring the liquid over the heat with a wooden spoon and scraping up the sediment gets all the flavor from the bottom of the pan to make a good sauce or gravy.

2

SOUPS

Soups provide an interesting and substantial first course without a great deal of effort. Armed with a food processor, all of these soups are very easy to make, especially the no-cook variety.

The secret of our soups lies in freshness and the quick release of flavors rather than long simmering. Many can simply be made with water, but a few call for stock and for this purpose a bouillon cube will not do. Use a good homemade stock or canned bouillon.

Many of these soups also make the most satisfying of light meals on their own, served with crusty bread or one of our "tartinis" (see pages 32–6) and perhaps followed by a salad or fruit and cheese.

Left: Shrimp Bisque (page 23); right: Quick Soup au Pistou (page 22)

NO-COOK SOUPS

These cold soups need no cooking and are incredibly quick to prepare. If the ingredients are cold enough the soups can simply be served as they are. For a chilled soup, add some ice cubes to the serving bowls or whizz them first in the food processor as the soup is made.

COLD CREAM of TOMATO SOUP with CHERVIL

🕐 *under 10 minutes*

If the tomatoes are really sweet there is no need for the sugar.

1 pound ripe tomatoes
1 teaspoon sugar
bunch of fresh chervil
$\frac{3}{4}$ cup light cream
salt and pepper

1 Whizz the tomatoes with the sugar in the food processor until they become light and frothy, snipping in half the chervil with the machine still running.

2 Pour into a large bowl and mix in just enough cream to give a thick but liquid consistency. Season to taste with salt and pepper.

3 Pour into individual bowls and snip the remaining chervil over the top of each bowl. Drop a few ice cubes in each bowl, if wished.

COLD AVOCADO, SPINACH, and SCALLION SOUP

🕐 *under 10 minutes*

Use only perfectly ripe avocados for this dish. Pick over the spinach leaves and trim off any thick stems, or buy packages of ready-washed and trimmed leaves.

2 large ripe avocados
1 lime
4 scallions
1 pound baby spinach leaves
$2\frac{1}{2}$ cups vegetable or chicken stock or water
dash of Worcestershire sauce
pinch of cayenne
salt and pepper

1 Halve, peel, and pit the avocados and then coarsely chop the flesh. Squeeze the juice from the lime and sprinkle a little over the avocado. Snip the scallions into short lengths.

2 In the food processor, whizz until smooth the avocados and scallions with the remaining lime juice and almost all the spinach leaves. Whizz in a little stock or water.

3 Pour into a large bowl and add just enough stock or water to get a thick but liquid consistency.

4 Season to taste with Worcestershire sauce, cayenne, and salt and pepper.

5 Pour into individual bowls and add a few ice cubes to each if you wish. Garnish with the reserved spinach leaves, finely snipped.

COLD FRESH HERB SOUP

🕐 *under 20 minutes*

You do need a good quality stock for this soup. Use any one of the herbs on their own or a mixture as preferred, depending on availability. Arugula and sorrel are also good in this dish.

1 quart vegetable or chicken stock
3 or 4 small handfuls of fresh herbs, including flat-leaf parsley, lemon thyme, basil, and tarragon
1 cup sour cream
salt and pepper

1 Whizz a little stock in the food processor with most of the herbs until they are well chopped.

2 Add $\frac{3}{4}$ cup of the sour cream and blend lightly, then pour into a tureen or large bowl. Stir in just enough of the remaining stock to give a good thick but liquid consistency.

3 Season the soup to taste and then pour into individual bowls.

4 Swirl the reserved sour cream on the tops of the bowls and garnish with the reserved herb sprigs.

Cold Fresh Herb Soup

 HOT SOUPS

The good fresh flavors of the ingredients are strong enough to allow these soups to be made using only water instead of stock. Time can be saved by heating the water in the microwave while processing the vegetables. Many of these soups are substantial enough to make good snack meals, served with crusty bread.

QUICK SOUPE au PISTOU

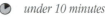 *under 20 minutes*

The pistou sauce for this version of a classic Provençal soup has many other uses and is particularly good with firm-fleshed fish, poultry, and steamed vegetables. It also makes a good pasta sauce.

1 quart of vegetable or chicken stock or water
1 pound ripe tomatoes
$\frac{2}{3}$ cup olive oil
4 scallions
1 pound fine green beans
1 large zucchini
2 cups canned cannellini or red kidney beans
6 ounces vermicelli
5 garlic cloves
bunch of fresh basil leaves
2 ounces Parmesan cheese
salt and pepper
2 ounces Swiss cheese

1 Bring the stock or water to a boil and coarsely chop the tomatoes.

2 Put one third of the oil in a large heavy saucepan and place over moderate heat. Snip in the scallions and cook a minute or two.

3 Add the tomatoes to the pan and cook another few minutes while preparing the other vegetables.

4 Trim the green beans and snip them into short lengths. Slice the zucchini.

5 Add the boiling stock or water to the pan followed by the prepared vegetables, the drained canned beans, and the vermicelli. Simmer gently about 10 minutes.

6 Meanwhile, make the pistou: peel the garlic cloves and put them in the food processor with the basil and half the Parmesan in pieces. Whizz to a coarse paste and then, with the machine still running, add the remaining oil in a steady stream. Season with salt and pepper.

7 Season the soup to taste and stir in the pistou just before serving.

8 Grate the remaining Parmesan and the Swiss cheese and serve separately, for sprinkling on the soup.

PEA and SMOKED HAM SOUP

 under 10 minutes

1 quart vegetable or chicken stock or water
2 tablespoons butter
4 scallions
1 pound frozen green peas
1 or 2 sprigs of fresh summer savory
$1\frac{1}{4}$ cups plain yogurt
salt and pepper
2 thick slices of smoked ham
small bunch of fresh chives

1 Bring the stock or water to a boil.

2 Melt the butter in a large heavy saucepan over moderate heat and snip in the scallions. Sauté a minute or two.

3 Add the peas and savory with a little of the stock or water and bring to a boil, then simmer a minute or two.

4 Whizz the mixture in the food processor until smooth. Return to the pan.

5 Mix in the yogurt and just enough of the remaining stock to give a good thick but liquid consistency. Season with pepper and a little salt if necessary.

6 Pour into bowls and snip over the ham and chives.

SHRIMP BISQUE

🕐 *under 20 minutes*

1 quart fish stock
1 fennel bulb
1 pound cooked shelled small shrimp
$1\frac{1}{2}$ tablespoons butter
4 scallions
handful of parsley
1 bay leaf
$\frac{3}{4}$ cup dry white wine
juice of 1 lemon
$1\frac{1}{4}$ cups whipping cream
1 tablespon brandy
salt and cayenne

1   Bring the stock to a boil. Remove the outer leaves and woody core from the fennel and chop it into small pieces, reserving the feathery leaves. Halve all but 12 small shrimp.

2   Melt the butter in a large heavy saucepan over moderate heat. Add the fennel to the pan and then snip in the scallions and parsley with its stems. Sauté about 3 minutes.

3   Add the bay leaf, wine, and lemon juice. Cook rapidly until syrupy. Remove the bay leaf and add the halved shrimp. Stir well and pour in a little of the boiling stock. Simmer 2 or 3 minutes.

4   Whizz the mixture in the food processor. Return the mixture to the pan, stir in the rest of the stock, and add the cream and brandy.

5   Season to taste with salt and cayenne and heat gently a minute or two. Garnish with the reserved shrimp and snip over the fennel fronds.

Variation:
If the shrimp don't have much color and the soup is very pale, add some tomato paste.

SWEET-AND-SOUR NOODLE SOUP

🕐 *under 10 minutes*

Try any one of the wide variety of noodles now available in larger supermarkets as well as Oriental grocers. If you use those which need only soaking, time may be saved in the final simmering.

1 quart vegetable or chicken stock or water
4 slices of bacon
piece of fresh ginger root about 1 inch thick
3 scallions
2 garlic cloves
1 tablespoon sugar
pinch of five-spice powder
$\frac{1}{4}$ pound oyster mushrooms
1 head Napa cabbage or romaine lettuce
1 tablespoon soy sauce
2 tablespoons wine vinegar
$\frac{1}{4}$ pound cellophane noodles
salt and pepper
1 tablespoon sesame oil

1   Bring the stock or water to a boil.

2   Put a large heavy saucepan over high heat and snip in the bacon. Dry-fry a minute or two.

3   Meanwhile, peel the ginger and put it in the food processor. Add the scallions, broken into pieces, followed by the peeled garlic. Process to a paste and add to the pan along with the sugar and five-spice powder. Stir-fry 1 minute.

4   Roughly chop the mushrooms and leaves and add to the pan with the soy sauce. Stir-fry 1 minute.

5   Pour in the boiling stock and the vinegar, break in the noodles, and simmer a few minutes.

6   Season to taste with salt and pepper, pour into individual bowls, and dribble a few drops of sesame oil over each.

CHICKEN and LEEK SOUP

🕐 *under 15 minutes*

1 quart vegetable or chicken stock or water
1½ tablespoons butter
2 sun-dried tomatoes in oil
4 scallions
1 stalk of celery
¼ pound skinless boneless chicken breast
2 leeks
¾ cup dry white wine
salt and pepper
small bunch of parsley

1 Bring the stock or water to a boil.

2 Melt the butter with 1 tablespoon of the oil from the sun-dried tomatoes over moderate heat in a large heavy saucepan. Snip in the scallions and the celery and cook 2 or 3 minutes.

3 Meanwhile, slice or shred the chicken into small strips and snip the sun-dried tomatoes. Trim and halve the leeks and rinse them under running water to remove any grit.

4 Add the chicken and sun-dried tomatoes to the pan, increase the heat slightly, and sauté 2 minutes, stirring frequently.

5 Shake off any excess moisture from the leeks and then snip them coarsely into the pan.

6 Sauté the contents of the pan until the leeks have just wilted.

7 Pour in the boiling stock or water and the wine and simmer gently about 5 minutes.

8 Season to taste, pour into warmed bowls, and snip over some parsley to serve.

POACHED SMOKED HADDOCK and EGG SOUP with MILK

🕐 *under 10 minutes*

You can also try poaching the eggs whole in the soup, until they are just set but still runny inside. Other smoked fish can also be used.

1 pound smoked haddock
1 quart whole milk
2 bay leaves
4 black peppercorns
4 eggs
1 tablespoon horseradish sauce
black pepper
pinch of cayenne

1 Put the fish in a pan and cover with the milk. Add the bay leaves and whole peppercorns. Bring to a boil and simmer gently about 5 minutes.

2 Remove the fish from the pan and let it cool slightly. Remove the skin and flake the flesh into the food processor.

3 Strain the milk and add a few spoonfuls to the fish. Whizz briefly to a coarse mixture, but do not over-process.

4 Put this mixture in a large saucepan and stir in the remaining strained milk. Bring to a boil over moderate heat, then reduce the heat to a simmer.

5 Beat the eggs lightly and stir them into the soup with the horseradish sauce. Simmer 2 or 3 minutes and then season to taste with pepper.

6 Pour into bowls and sprinkle each lightly with cayenne to serve.

CANNELLINI BEAN, GARLIC, and CURLY ENDIVE SOUP

🕐 *under 10 minutes*

1 quart vegetable or chicken stock
⅓ cup olive oil
3 garlic cloves, minced
1 small head of curly endive
1 can (15-ounce) of cannellini beans
salt and pepper

1 Bring the stock to a boil.

2 Heat half the oil in a large heavy saucepan over moderate heat and then add the garlic. Sauté about 3 minutes.

3 Meanwhile, snip the curly endive leaves into small pieces and drain the beans.

4 Add the endive shreds to the pan, reserving a few, and cook gently until the leaves are just wilted, then add the beans.

5 Stir in the boiling stock and bring back to a boil. Simmer gently about 5 minutes.

6 Adjust the seasoning. Just before serving, trickle in the remaining oil and finely snip over the reserved endive leaves.

Cannellini Bean, Garlic, and Curly Endive Soup

3

Appetizers,
Snacks
and LIGHT MEALS

There are in this chapter dozens of interesting recipes for first courses or snack lunches that are very simple to make either in the middle of a busy day or while preparing a main course. Cooking most of them takes no longer than reheating an expensive ready-cooked meal that you have purchased.

Many people today are turning to meals which consist of two appetizers or light dishes, and most of ours are also easily scaled up to make substantial main courses in their own right. As a rule of thumb, just double the ingredients. In the egg dishes, for instance, use two eggs per person, rather than one.

Pasta is particularly versatile, easily adjusted for small or large numbers, and makes a fine supper-party main course when served with a large salad.

Left: Grilled Radicchio with Goat Cheese (page 28); right: rigatoni with Poached Baby Vegetables (page 42)

BRESAOLA with SHAVED PARMESAN and OLIVE OIL

🕐 *under 10 minutes*

Bresaola is dried salt beef from the Lombardy region of Italy. It may be obtained from Italian delis or ready-sliced in packs from good supermarkets.

2-ounce chunk of Parmesan cheese
6 tablespoons extra-virgin olive oil
1 tablespon lemon juice
pepper
12 thin slices of bresaola
small bunch of flat-leaf parsley

1   Shave the cheese into thin slivers. Mix the oil and lemon juice in a bowl and season with pepper.

2   Arrange 3 slices of bresaola on each plate and pour the dressing over them.

3   Place 2 or 3 slivers of cheese over the meat on each plate.

4   Season with some more pepper and snip over the parsley.

CARROTS VINAIGRETTE

🕐 *under 10 minutes*

Use baby carrots if available; otherwise coarsely chop larger ones.

$\frac{3}{4}$ pound young carrots
3 scallions
$\frac{1}{2}$ orange
$\frac{1}{3}$ cup olive oil
1 tablespoon sherry vinegar
salt and pepper
2 or 3 sprigs cilantro
2 tablespoons pine nuts

1   Rinse the carrots and shred them in the food processor, using the shredding blade. Put into a salad bowl and snip over the scallions.

2   Grate 1 teaspoon of zest from the orange and squeeze 1 tablespoon of juice.

3   Mix the oil and vinegar together with the orange zest and juice. Season to taste with salt and pepper and pour over the salad.

4   Snip over the cilantro, sprinkle over the pine nuts, and toss well to coat all the ingredients with the dressing.

GRILLED RADICCHIO with GOAT CHEESE

🕐 *under 10 minutes*

For this sort of treatment use one of the logs of factory-made goat cheese which are more economical. Cut it in slices about $\frac{1}{4}$ inch thick.

2 small heads of radicchio
4 thick slices of fresh goat cheese
2 tablespoons olive oil
6 fresh basil leaves
2 or 3 sprigs of fresh thyme
salt and pepper

1   Preheat the broiler.

2   Cut the radicchio heads lengthwise in halves and take out a few of the center leaves to create a hollow. Arrange the radicchio, cut side up, on 4 flameproof dishes.

3   Put a slice of cheese in each cavity and brush the leaves and cheese with the oil.

4   Snip over the basil and thyme. Season with pepper and a little salt on the leaves only.

5   Broil until the cheese is bubbling.

WARM MUSHROOMS à LA GRECQUE

🕐 *under 10 minutes*

This treatment also works very well with drained canned artichoke hearts instead of mushrooms.

1 pound mushrooms
1 teaspoon coriander seeds
1 garlic clove
3 tablespoons olive oil
$\frac{1}{2}$ teaspoon ground cumin
2 tablespoons white wine
salt and pepper
2 or 3 sprigs of flat-leaf parsley
2 or 3 sprigs cilantro

1   Wipe the mushrooms and halve or slice them if they are large. Lightly crush the coriander seeds.

2   Rub a sauté pan with the garlic clove. Heat the oil in it over moderate heat and add the cumin and coriander seeds. Sauté 1 minute, then add the mushrooms. Sauté another 3–4 minutes, stirring frequently.

3   Add the wine and cook 1 or 2 minutes more over high heat.

4   Season to taste with salt and pepper. Snip over the parsley and coriander leaves, mix well, and serve.

STIR-FRIED EGGS with SHRIMP and SNOW PEAS

🕐 *under 10 minutes*

The secret of this dish is light cooking. Do not overcook the eggs – they should be just set but still slightly moist.

$\frac{1}{4}$ pound snow peas
$\frac{1}{2}$ lemon
6 ounces shelled cooked small shrimp
1 tablespoon oil
3 scallions
$\frac{1}{2}$ teaspoon soy sauce
4 eggs
salt and pepper

1   Top and tail the snow peas. Squeeze the juice from the lemon and toss the shrimp in it.

2   In a frying pan or wok, heat the oil over moderate to high heat and snip in the scallions. Stir fry 1–2 minutes then snip in the snow peas in $\frac{1}{2}$-inch chunks. Cook 2 more minutes.

3   Drain the shrimp and add them with the soy sauce. Stir-fry 1 minute only.

4   Beat the eggs lightly with 2 tablespoons of water and some salt and pepper and pour into the wok. Stir-fry until the eggs are just firm but still moist, then serve.

EGGS en COCOTTE with SPINACH

🕐 *under 15 minutes*

4 tablespoons butter
2 ounces fresh young spinach leaves
large pinch of grated nutmeg
$\frac{1}{4}$ cup light cream
salt and pepper
4 eggs
1 tablespoon grated Parmesan cheese

1   Heat the oven to 350°F.

2   Use half the butter to coat the sides and bottoms of 4 ramekins or custard cups.

3   Into each ramekin snip some spinach and sprinkle some nutmeg. Then trickle in 1 tablespoon of cream into each and season with salt and pepper. Break an egg into each.

4   Dot the top of each ramekin with the remaining butter, sprinkle with the cheese, and place them in a deep-sided baking dish.

5   Pour enough boiling water into the baking dish to come at least halfway up the sides of the ramekins.

6   Bake 7-10 minutes, depending on how well set you want the eggs to be.

Variations:
1   There are innumerable variations on this classic dish: Try replacing the spinach with watercress, chives, sorrel, or sautéed sliced mushrooms.

2   Instead of vegetables, use grated cheese, flaked smoked fish, or strips of smoked salmon as flavoring additions.

BABY CAULIFLOWERS in STILTON SAUCE

🕐 *under 15 minutes*

If baby cauliflowers are not available, divide a large firm head into 4, removing the woody core.

4 baby cauliflowers
3 tablespoons butter
$\frac{1}{4}$ cup flour
1 cup milk
6 ounces Stilton or other good blue cheese
2 tablespoons port
salt and pepper
pinch of cayenne

1   Take off most of the outside leaves of the cauliflowers, trim their bases, and cut a deep cross into them.

2   Put them in a large pan, sprinkle lightly with salt, and cover them with boiling water. Place over high heat and bring to a boil, then cover and simmer gently until just tender, about 10 minutes.

3   Meanwhile, melt the butter in a saucepan over moderate heat and add the flour. Stir with a wooden spoon to mix into a roux and cook 2-3 minutes until smooth and just beginning to color.

4   Gradually add the milk and cook, stirring, a few minutes until thick and smooth.

5   Off the heat, crumble in the cheese, add the port, and season to taste. Mix well until the cheese has all melted.

6   Drain the cooked cauliflowers well and place one on each of 4 plates. Pour the sauce over them and sprinkle very lightly with cayenne.

SMOKED EEL FILLETS with APPLE and MUSTARD SAUCE

🕐 *under 10 minutes*

If the eel fillets are small allow 2 per person.

1 tablespoon olive oil
2 scallions
2 firm tart apples
$\frac{1}{2}$ lemon
$\frac{1}{4}$ cup sour cream
2 tablespoons whole-grain mustard
2 tablespoons horseradish sauce
salt and pepper
small bunch of fresh dill or arugula
4 smoked eel fillets

1   Heat the oil in a sauté pan over moderate heat. Snip in the scallions and sauté 1 or 2 minutes.

2   Meanwhile, halve the apples and core them. Then grate or chop them coarsely. Squeeze the juice from the lemon.

3   Add the apples to the pan with the cream, mustard, horseradish, and 1 or 2 tablespoons of the lemon juice. Season to taste with salt and pepper. Snip in most of the dill or arugula and cook gently 1 or 2 minutes.

4   Pour the sauce on 4 plates and place a smoked eel fillet in the middle of each. Dribble a little more lemon juice over each fillet and snip over the reserved dill or arugula.

PAPAYA with SMOKED MACKEREL MOUSSE

🕐 *under 10 minutes*

Use only perfectly ripe papayas and, if possible, try to chill them beforehand for better flavor and easier preparation.

$\frac{3}{4}$ pound skinned smoked mackerel fillets
$\frac{1}{2}$ cup crème fraîche or sour cream
$\frac{1}{4}$ cup horseradish sauce
1 teaspoon tomato paste
1 lemon
2 or 3 drops Tabasco sauce
salt and pepper
2 ripe papayas

1   Flake the fish fillets into the food processor. Add the cream, horseradish, tomato paste, and the juice of half the lemon. Whizz until smooth. Season to taste with the Tabasco, salt and pepper. Whizz again briefly to mix.

2   Peel and halve the papayas. Remove their seeds and halve each half again into quarters.

3   On each plate put a mound of the mousse and then place 2 quarters of papaya side by side, concave sides around the mousse to sandwich it closely so that there is a thick band of filling between them.

4   Sprinkle with the juice of the remaining lemon half to serve.

Jumbo Shrimp Sautéed with Ginger and Chili

JUMBO SHRIMP SAUTÉED with GINGER and CHILI

🕐 *under 10 minutes*

12 cooked jumbo shrimp in shell
piece of fresh ginger root about $\frac{1}{2}$ inch across
2 garlic cloves
1 small fresh chili pepper
1 lemon
2 tablespoons sunflower oil
2 tablespoons sesame oil
salt and pepper

1 Rinse the shrimp and pat them dry. If preferred, twist off their tails.

2 Peel the ginger and garlic. Cut the chili pepper in half and remove its seeds.

3 Whizz the garlic, ginger, and chili in the food processor. Add the juice from the lemon with half the sunflower oil and whizz again briefly.

4 Heat the sesame oil and the remaining sunflower oil in a sauté pan or wok over moderate heat.

5 Add the ginger and chili mixture and stir-fry about 2 or 3 minutes.

6 Add the shrimp and stir fry another 2 minutes. Season and serve.

Variation:
To make these into canapés, use shelled jumbo shrimp. Fry 3 slices of bread in 1 tablespoon of sesame oil with a small pat of butter and 2 tablespoons of sesame seeds. Cut each slice into 4 triangles and serve each of the shrimp on one, coated with the pan juices and sesame seeds.

TARTINIS

As baking is the one thing you cannot do in a matter of minutes, we have made a point of devising several snacks and appetizers using the wide range of flavored breads, biscuits, and muffins now so readily available. Our "tartini" is a cross between the French tartine, *or open sandwich, and the Italian* crostini, *or toasted open sandwich.*

MOZZARELLA, ANCHOVY, and CAPERS on TOAST

under 15 minutes

1 2-ounce can of flat anchovies in oil
8 slices of crusty white bread
2 tablespoons capers
6 ounces mozzarella cheese
pepper

1 Heat the broiler. Drain the anchovies, reserving their oil, and halve or cut them into small lengths.

2 Toast the bread on one side under the broiler.

3 Brush the untoasted side with the oil from the anchovies, arrange the anchovy fillets on top, and sprinkle each with a few capers.

4 Slice the cheese fairly thinly and arrange over the bread. Sprinkle with pepper.

5 Broil until very hot and the cheese is bubbling.

Variation:
Onion bread is also good in this dish.

BABY TOMATO and PESTO MINI PIZZAS

under 15 minutes

Use "passata", the Italian tomato purée, if possible.

4 ciabatta or other Italian rolls
$\frac{1}{4}$ pound mozzarella cheese
6 ounces cherry tomatoes
1 garlic clove
1 tablespoon olive oil
$\frac{1}{4}$ cup tomato purée
$\frac{1}{2}$ cup pesto sauce
salt and pepper
about 16 fresh basil leaves

1 Heat the broiler.

2 Cut the rolls across in halves and thinly slice the mozzarella. Halve the cherry tomatoes and mince the garlic.

3 In a bowl, mix the olive oil, tomato purée, garlic, and pesto sauce. Season to taste with pepper.

4 Spread this mixture over the roll halves and cover with the mozzarella slices. Dot with the halved tomatoes.

5 Broil until the cheese is bubbling.

6 Snip over the basil leaves and sprinkle with more pepper to serve.

Variation:
Use a purchased pizza base and cut with a cookie cutter to get the right size.

ASPARAGUS TIPS and ANCHOVY on ENGLISH MUFFINS

under 10 minutes

8 anchovy fillets
1 tablespoon capers
6 tablespoons olive oil
1 lemon
salt and pepper
4 English muffins
1 cup canned asparagus tips

1 Heat the broiler. Drain and wipe the anchovies to take off some of the salt.

2 Snip them into the food processor with the capers, oil, the juice of half the lemon, and some pepper. Whizz to a smooth paste.

3 Split the muffins in half, toast them lightly, and spread them thickly with the paste. Drain the asparagus tips well and then arrange them on the muffin halves.

4 Sprinkle with a little more lemon juice and pepper. Heat through again briefly under the broiler.

Variations:
1 Use fresh asparagus tips, steamed lightly about 3 minutes or blanched 2 minutes.

2 Hard-cook an egg while making this tartini, then shell it and grate it over the asparagus.

Top: Baby Tomato and Pesto Mini Pizzas; Bottom: Asparagus Tips and Anchovy on English Muffins

CREAM of MUSHROOM MUFFINS

under 20 minutes

This is even tastier with a few wild mushrooms.

$\frac{1}{4}$ pound mushrooms
4 tablespoons butter
salt and pepper
4 English muffins
$\frac{1}{4}$ cup white wine
$\frac{3}{4}$ cup crème fraîche or heavy cream
pinch of freshly grated nutmeg
small bunch of fresh chives

1 Heat the broiler. Slice the mushrooms, or halve them if small.

2 Melt one-third of the butter in a sauté pan over moderate to high heat and add the mushrooms with some seasoning. Sauté until they give off their liquid.

3 While the mushrooms are cooking, split the muffins and toast them lightly under the broiler.

4 Remove the cooked mushrooms with a slotted spoon and keep warm. Add the wine to the sauté pan and reduce over high heat until only 1 or 2 tablespoons of liquid are left.

5 Stir in the cream and reduce again until it has a good thick consistency. Beat in the remaining butter and then add a little nutmeg and adjust the seasoning, if necessary.

6 Spread a little of the cream sauce on the toasted muffin halves.

7 Return the mushrooms to the pan and mix well with the remaining sauce.

8 Spoon the mushroom cream on the muffin halves, snip over the chives, and serve.

GUACAMOLE on WALNUT BREAD

under 10 minutes

The guacamole also makes a very good dip. Serve it with tortilla chips.

2 small fresh green chili peppers
4 scallions
2 or 3 sprigs cilantro
2 firm ripe tomatoes
2 large ripe avocados
1 lime
salt and pepper
4 slices of walnut bread

1 Halve the chilis and remove their seeds. Snip them into the bowl of the food processor, followed by the scallions and cilantro.

2 Chop the tomatoes coarsely. Peel, seed, and coarsely chop the avocados.

3 Add both to the food processor with the juice of half the lime. Whizz until just smooth, but still with a bit of texture.

4 Season to taste with salt and pepper and add a little more lime juice, if necessary, but do not make it too liquid.

5 Cut the walnut bread slices in halves or quarters and spread the guacamole thickly on them.

Variation:
If you can't get walnut bread, onion bread works equally well.

GRAVLAX and CRÈME FRAÎCHE on RYE BREAD

under 10 minutes

$\frac{3}{4}$ cup crème fraîche or sour cream
1 tablespoon sweet mustard, preferably dill
    mustard
$\frac{1}{2}$ lemon
salt and pepper
4 slices of rye bread
white parts only 2 scallions
$\frac{1}{4}$ pound gravlax
small sprig of fresh dill leaves

1 In a bowl, mix the cream with the mustard and 1 or 2 tablespoons of lemon juice. Do not add too much lemon juice or the sauce will become too runny. Season to taste with salt and pepper.

2 Cut the slices of bread across diagonally into triangles and snip the scallions over them. Spoon two-thirds of the cream mixture over them and then arrange the gravlax on top.

3 Spoon the remaining cream mixture in large dollops on top of the gravlax. Snip the dill over the tops.

BRUSCHETTA with CIABATTA

🕐 *under 10 minutes*

This is an excellent way of using up very ripe squashy tomatoes.

1 loaf of ciabatta or other Italian bread
2 garlic cloves
2 tablespoons olive oil
1 very ripe large tomato
salt and pepper
2-ounce piece Parmesan cheese

1 Heat the broiler.

2 Halve the loaf lengthwise and toast lightly on both sides under the broiler.

3 Rub the cut surfaces with the garlic and then brush with the oil.

4 Halve the tomato. Smear one half over each piece of bread, spreading the pulp on it.

5 Season and grate over the Parmesan.

6 Return to the broiler briefly until the cheese melts, then cut each piece of bread across in half to serve.

Left to right: Gravlax and Crème Fraîche on Rye Bread, Potato Cakes with Bacon and Blue Cheese (page 36) and Guacamole on Walnut Bread

POTATO CAKES *with* BACON *and* BLUE CHEESE

🕐 *under 15 minutes*

If potato cakes are unavailable use English muffins, pita bread or bagels.

6 ounces blue cheese
4 slices of bacon
4 potato cakes
freshly ground black pepper
pinch of cayenne

1 Heat the broiler and cut the cheese in slices.

2 Broil the bacon until well cooked on both sides.

3 About halfway through the cooking, put the cakes under the broiler with the bacon and toast one side of them until lightly colored.

4 Brush the untoasted side lightly with a little of the bacon fat from the broiler pan.

5 Cut each slice of bacon in two and arrange them in pairs on each cake, then cover with blue cheese.

6 Season with pepper and broil until the cheese is bubbling.

7 Sprinkle lightly with cayenne and serve cut across in half.

HERBY SCRAMBLED EGGS *on* MUFFINS

🕐 *under 10 minutes*

4 tablespoons butter
8 eggs
2 tablespoons light cream
few drops Worcestershire sauce
$\frac{1}{4}$ cup finely snipped mixed fresh herbs, preferably parsley, savory, thyme, chives, or tarragon
salt and pepper
4 English muffins

1 Melt two-thirds of the butter in a heavy pan over low heat.

2 Break the eggs into a small bowl and beat them lightly. Stir in the cream, Worcestershire sauce, most of the herbs, and salt and pepper to taste.

3 Pour the mixture into the pan and cook, stirring, until the eggs are just beginning to set.

4 While the eggs are cooking, split the muffins and toast them lightly. Spread the halves with a little of the remaining butter.

5 Spoon the eggs on the muffin halves, put a small pat of butter on each, and sprinkle lightly with the reserved herbs.

STIR-FRIED SCALLION *and* PROSCIUTTO CROÛTES

🕐 *under 10 minutes*

The scallion and prosciutto mixture also makes the basis of a good salad. Toss it with watercress or lambs' lettuce (mâche).

2 tablespoons olive oil
2 garlic cloves
12 leafy scallions
small sprig of fresh lemon thyme
$\frac{1}{2}$ lemon
salt and pepper
4 thin slices of prosciutto
4 thick slices of crusty white Italian bread

1 Put the oil in a sauté pan over low to moderate heat and mince the garlic into it. Cook 1 or 2 minutes.

2 Turn up the heat to high and snip the scallions into the pan in 2-inch lengths, followed by the lemon thyme and the juice of the lemon. Season well with salt and pepper.

3 Put the prosciutto slices on top of each other, roll them into a cylinder, and then snip this in narrow strips into the pan.

4 Sauté a few minutes until the scallions are just tender but still slightly crunchy. Season.

5 Arrange the mixture on the slices of bread to serve.

● *PASTA*

Pasta is a great standby for the quick cook. You can keep a wide variety of dried pasta in the kitchen cupboard and make your own sauce in a matter of minutes – some do not even require cooking and are simply stirred into the cooked and drained pasta. Always take the time to grate any accompanying Parmesan freshly. Purchased grated cheese has little of the taste or pungency of the original.

BASIC RECIPE *for* COOKING PASTA

◗ *under 15 minutes*

The exact cooking time of dried pasta will depend on the type and thickness of the pasta as well as its age. Start testing after the shortest time given on the package: The pasta should be just tender but still firm to the bite. Fresh pasta, of course, cooks in a matter of minutes. Speed up the process by heating some of the water in the microwave.

1 pound dried pasta
2 tablespoons salt
1 or 2 tablespoons olive oil

1   Put $4\frac{1}{2}$ quarts of water in a large pot and put over high heat. Add the salt and 1 tablespoon of oil to the water in the pot.

2   While the water is heating start making the sauce.

3   When the water is boiling rapidly, put in the pasta. If it is in long strands like spaghetti, break the strands cleanly in half, in handfuls, before adding it to the water. Bring back to a good rolling boil and cook rapidly until the pasta is tender but still firm to the bite.

4   Drain the cooked pasta well.

5   If using a no-cook sauce, return the drained pasta to the pan and stir the sauce into it over low heat for a minute or so. Otherwise, stir the remaining oil into the drained pasta to keep the strands from sticking together, put it in a warmed serving dish, and pour the sauce over it.

NO·COOK SAUCES

These sauces are very quickly prepared and are simply stirred into the pasta after it has been drained and returned to the pan over low heat. This is sufficient to warm the sauce through or cook it slightly should that be necessary. For instructions on cooking the pasta please see page 37.

QUICK CARBONARA

🕐   *under 10 minutes*

2 eggs
$\frac{3}{4}$ cup light cream
2-ounce piece Parmesan cheese
salt and pepper
2 slices of prosciutto
1 thick slice of smoked ham
2 or 3 sprigs of flat-leaf parsley

1   In a large bowl, lightly beat the eggs and then mix in the cream.

2   Grate in the Parmesan and season to taste. Snip in the meats and parsley.

3   Put the cooked and drained pasta back in the pan. Add the sauce and toss well over low heat to coat the pasta thoroughly with the mixture.

CRUSHED NUT VINAIGRETTE

🕐   *under 15 minutes*

This sauce, based on a classic Italian dish, goes especially well with thin noodles. such as spaghettini or vermicelli, and is best served without any accompanying cheese. You can vary the nuts according to preference and, if you have the time, toasting the almonds produces a memorable flavor.

$\frac{1}{4}$ cup shelled blanched almonds
$\frac{1}{4}$ cup shelled pistachios
2 garlic cloves
3 tablespoons olive oil
1 tablespoon walnut oil
1 tablespoon lemon juice
salt and pepper
$\frac{1}{4}$ cup pine nuts
2 or 3 sprigs of parsley
5 or 6 fresh basil leaves

1   Put the almonds and pistachios in the food processor with the peeled garlic and whizz briefly until coarsely chopped. Do not over-process.

2   In a cup or small bowl, mix the olive oil and the walnut oil with the lemon juice and salt and pepper to taste.

3   Pour the vinaigrette over the cooked and drained pasta returned to the pan over low heat and mix well to coat thoroughly.

4   Sprinkle in the crushed nut mixture and the whole pine nuts and snip over the herbs. Toss well again and serve.

SALAMI, PARSLEY, and OLIVES

🕐   *under 10 minutes*

Use a good strong Italian salami for this dish, or try some of the more exotic varieties, such as those made from wild boar or studded with pistachio nuts. A light pink salami looks very good against green pasta. Garlic-flavored olives give the best result.

12 thick slices of salami
3 or 4 sprigs of flat-leaf parsley
$\frac{3}{4}$ cup pitted black olives
2 tablespoons olive oil
pepper

1   Cut the slices of salami into strips. Into a bowl, snip these strips into cubes. Then snip in the parsley and olives.

2   Pour the oil over the cooked and drained pasta returned to the pan. Then scatter over the contents of the the bowl and season generously with pepper. Mix in well over low heat.

Spaghettini verdi with Salami, Parsley, and Olives

TOMATO and FENNEL

🕐 *under 10 minutes*

½ fennel bulb, with plenty of feathery tops
1 pound ripe tomatoes
1 scallion
1 garlic clove
2 tablespoons olive oil
salt and pepper
pinch of sugar (optional)

1 Take off the outer stalks from the fennel, remove the woody core, and reserve the feathery leaves.

2 Whizz the tomatoes, fennel, scallion, and peeled garlic together in the food processor until coarsely chopped.

3 Mix in just enough olive oil to give the sauce a good thick consistency and season well. Add a little sugar, if necessary.

4 Mix the sauce into the cooked and drained pasta returned to the pan over low heat. Snip over the reserved fennel leaves.

SMOKED SALMON, SOUR CREAM, and CHIVES

🕐 *under 15 minutes*

This sauce goes best with thin noodles, such as spaghettini.

1 lemon
1¼ cups sour cream
pepper
1 scallion
¼ pound smoked salmon
bunch of fresh chives

1 In a bowl, mix the juice of half the lemon into the cream along with some pepper. Snip in the scallion and mix well.

2 Into another bowl, snip the salmon into thin strips about ¾ inch long.

3 Pour the cream mixture over the cooked and drained pasta returned to the pan and mix in well over low heat.

4 Scatter over the salmon and snip in the chives.

5 Toss well and serve with the remaining half lemon cut in wedges.

COOKED SAUCES

Apart from the Quick Bolognese, all of these sauces can be made in about the time it takes to cook the pasta itself. For instructions on cooking the pasta please see page 37.

WILTED SPINACH LEAVES and BACON

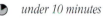 *under 10 minutes*

2 thick slices of smoked bacon
1 garlic clove
$\frac{1}{2}$ pound fresh baby spinach leaves
2 tablespoons oil
1 teaspoon soy sauce
pepper

1 Snip the bacon into a nonstick skillet and fry until crisp. Remove the bacon.

2 Mince the garlic, put it in the pan, and sauté 1 or 2 minutes, stirring frequently.

3 Snip handfuls of the spinach leaves into the pan in large shreds. Sauté over fairly high heat until the spinach is just wilted, stirring frequently.

4 Reduce the heat and stir in the oil and soy sauce. Snip in the cooked bacon and season with pepper.

5 Stir into the cooked and drained pasta.

LEEK and CHEDDAR

under 10 minutes

A few halved baby leeks also work very well in this dish.

1 large leek
$\frac{1}{4}$ pound Cheddar cheese
2 tablespoons olive oil
1 teaspoon Dijon-style mustard
$\frac{1}{2}$ lemon
2 tablespoons light cream
pinch of grated nutmeg
3 or 4 sprigs of parsley

1 Halve the leek and rinse it well under running water to remove any grit. Pat it dry and shred it. Coarsely shred the cheese.

2 Heat the oil in a sauté pan over moderate heat and sauté the shredded leek in it until just softened, 1–2 minutes.

3 Stir in the mustard, the juice of the half lemon, the cream, and nutmeg and cook another minute.

4 Stir the sauce into the drained and cooked pasta, sprinkle in the cheese, and toss well, then snip over the parsley.

SHRIMP, SUGAR PEAS and CHILI OIL

under 10 minutes

This sauce is best suited to round noodles or thinner pasta. If sugar peas are unobtainable, snow peas work equally well.

6 ounces sugar snap peas
1 garlic clove
3 tablespoons chili oil
1 tablespoon sherry vinegar
6 ounces shelled cooked small shrimp
salt and pepper

1 Cut the peas into short lengths and mince the garlic.

2 Heat the oil in a sauté pan over moderate heat. Add the garlic to the pan and sauté 1 or 2 minutes, stirring frequently.

3 Add the peas and the vinegar. Sauté 3 or 4 minutes, then add the shrimp and sauté 1 minute more.

4 Season to taste and stir into the cooked and drained pasta.

QUICK BOLOGNESE

◑ *under 30 minutes*

The better the quality of the ground steak, the better this sauce will be.

2 ounces bacon slices
1 scallion
1 stalk of celery
1 garlic clove, minced
$\frac{1}{2}$ pound ground steak
$\frac{1}{2}$ cup red wine
1 cup canned crushed tomatoes
3 or 4 sprigs of flat-leaf parsley
$\frac{1}{2}$ teaspoon Worcestershire sauce
2 teaspoons tomato paste
$\frac{1}{2}$ tablespoon dried oregano
salt and pepper

1   Heat a large sauté pan over moderate heat. Snip in the bacon, scallion, and celery and add the garlic. Cook 2 or 3 minutes, stirring frequently.

2   Turn up the heat to high, add the meat, and mix well. Press the mixture down into a flat cake and cook until the meat on the underside is well browned and beginning to stick to the pan.

3   Break up the cake, turning the meat, and then re-form it and repeat the process. Do this once more, or until the meat is uniformly browned.

4   Add the wine, mix well, and boil until the wine is mostly evaporated.

5   Add the tomatoes with their liquid and snip in the parsley. Add the Worcestershire sauce, tomato paste, and oregano. Season and mix well. Bring to a boil, and simmer rapidly 10 minutes.

POACHED BABY VEGETABLES

◑ *under 10 minutes*

Use a wide variety of tiny baby vegetables in this sauce, as long as they are fresh and tender. Cherry tomatoes and florets of young broccoli also work well.

$\frac{1}{2}$ pound tiny baby carrots
$\frac{1}{2}$ pound baby corn
$\frac{1}{2}$ pound baby green beans
$\frac{1}{2}$ pound baby zucchini
$\frac{1}{2}$ cup olive oil
2 tablespoons balsamic vinegar
4 or 5 sprigs of flat-leaf parsley
salt and pepper

1   Put $\frac{1}{4}$ inch of water in a wide saucepan and add a large pinch of salt. Put in all the vegetables, in a single layer if possible, cover the pan tightly, and bring to a boil.

2   Simmer until the vegetables are just tender, but still crunchy, 3–4 minutes.

3   While the vegetables are cooking, mix the oil and vinegar and snip in the parsley. Season to taste.

4   Drain the vegetables, put them into a warmed bowl and pour the vinaigrette over them. Mix well and then stir into the cooked and drained pasta.

CHICKEN LIVERS and CELERY

◑ *under 10 minutes*

$\frac{1}{2}$ pound chicken livers
2 stalks of celery
2 tablespoons oil
1 scallion
1 garlic clove
2 or 3 sprigs of parsley
2 tablespoons port or Madeira
6 tablespoons heavy cream
cayenne
salt and pepper

1   Trim and slice the chicken livers. Rinse them and pat dry. Trim off any coarse fibers from the celery stalks and chop them into fine strips.

2   Heat the oil in a sauté pan over moderate heat

3   Snip in the scallion. Mince the garlic and add it. Snip over most of the parsley and add the celery. Sauté 1–2 minutes.

4   Add the chicken livers and sauté a few minutes, depending on how pink you want the livers to be.

5   Add the wine and sauté a minute or so more to reduce it.

6   Stir in the cream, season to taste with cayenne, salt and pepper, and heat gently to warm through.

7   Stir into the cooked and drained pasta and snip over the remaining parsley.

TUNA FISH, RED ONION, and OLIVE OIL

🕐 *under 10 minutes*

The red onion is essential for this dish; yellow onions will not give the same result. If you do not have any lemon mayonnaise, finely grate some lemon zest into ordinary mayonnaise.

1 red onion
2 tablespoons olive oil
1 can (7-ounce) tuna fish in oil
$\frac{1}{2}$ lemon
1 tablespoon capers
2 tablespoons lemon mayonnaise
salt and pepper

1 Slice the onion into thin rings.

2 Heat the oil in a sauté pan over moderate heat and cook the onion in it 1–2 minutes.

3 Drain the tuna fish and flake the flesh into the pan. Add the juice from the lemon, along with the capers, mayonnaise, and salt and pepper to taste.

4 Cook another 2 or 3 minutes, stirring frequently, to warm the fish through, and then pour over the cooked and drained pasta.

Conchiglie with Tuna Fish, Red Onion, and Olive Oil

4

M AIN COURSES

Our main courses are mostly hot and based on fish, meat, and poultry, although there are also some main course salads in the next chapter. To cook at speed it is generally wisest to spend that little bit extra on prime quality cuts which are the most tender and best suit quick cooking. Also, ready-prepared fish and meats, although again more expensive, cut down drastically on preparation times.

For many of our main courses the greater part of the work is in the initial stages so that the dish can be left to finish, often covered with a lid, while the first course is being enjoyed.

Lamb Chops with Apricot, Cumin, and Garlic Sauce (page 62) accompanied by Baby New Potatoes (page 72) with Orange and Lemon Butter (page 51)

● *STRIPS*

Tender cuts of meat and poultry and firm-fleshed fish cook very quickly when sliced into thin strips. Start by cutting the meat into slices about $\frac{1}{4}$ inch thick and then cut these across into pieces about 2–3 inches long and 1 inch wide. Try to cut with the grain as this helps make the strips more tender, gives a better texture, and reduces shrinkage during cooking. Strips are best cooked by either sautéing them or stir-frying them in a wok. Make sure the pan is hot enough when they go in to seal the meat quickly so that it keeps its juices.

VEAL STRIPS with MUSTARD CREAM SAUCE

🕐 *under 10 minutes*

1 pound veal scaloppine
2 tablespoons butter
1 tablespoon oil
1 scallion
1 garlic clove, minced
1 teaspoon white wine vinegar
6 tablespoons light cream
1 tablespoon whole-grain mustard
1 teaspoon sweet or honey mustard
salt and pepper
pinch of paprika

1 Cut the veal into strips.

2 Melt the butter with the oil in a wok over moderate to high heat. Snip in the scallion and add the garlic. Stir-fry 1 or 2 minutes.

3 Add the veal strips and stir-fry 2 or 3 minutes.

4 Add the vinegar and stir-fry until it is almost all evaporated, 1–2 minutes.

5 Reduce the heat. Stir in the cream and mustards. Cook gently until warmed through, season to taste, and sprinkle with paprika to serve.

BEEF STRIPS with TOMATOES and HORSERADISH

🕐 *under 10 minutes*

Horseradish sauces and creams come in widely differing degrees of potency, so add them with caution.

1 pound filet mignon
$\frac{1}{2}$ pound ripe tomatoes
4 shallots
1 tablespoon red wine vinegar
2 tablespoons creamed horseradish
salt and pepper
4 tablespoons butter
2 tablespoons oil

1 Cut the beef into strips. Coarsely chop the tomatoes and shallots and whizz them in the food processor until smooth. Add the vinegar and horseradish and season to taste.

2 Melt half the butter with half the oil in a wok over moderate to high heat and cook the sauce, stirring, 2 or 3 minutes. Tip out into a warmed bowl and keep hot.

3 Add the remaining butter and oil to the wok and stir-fry the beef strips until well browned.

4 Lower the heat and return the sauce to the wok. Simmer gently 1–2 minutes. Adjust the seasoning, if necessary.

PORK STRIPS with PIZZAIOLA SAUCE

under 15 minutes

The pizzaiola sauce works equally well with beef and poultry.

1 pound pork tenderloin
2 green bell peppers
1 pound ripe tomatoes
1 tablespoon oil
3 scallions
2 garlic cloves
2 ounces mushrooms
2 teaspoons chopped fresh oregano
3 or 4 drops of Tabasco sauce
salt and pepper

1 Cut the pork into strips. Halve and seed the bell peppers. Coarsely chop the tomatoes.

2 Heat the oil in the wok over high heat. Add the pork strips and bell peppers and stir-fry 3 or 4 minutes.

3 Reduce the heat slightly. Snip in the scallions and mince in the garlic. Stir-fry 1 or 2 minutes.

4 Snip the mushrooms into the pan in thin strips and cook 1 or 2 minutes more.

5 Add the tomatoes and oregano and bring to a simmer. Add the pepper sauce and season to taste with salt and pepper. Cover and cook gently about 5 minutes.

SALMON STRIPS with CUCUMBER and CRÈME FRAÎCHE

under 10 minutes

This dish is better if the cucumber is left unpeeled.

1 pound salmon scaloppine (thin slices of fillet)
$\frac{1}{2}$ large cucumber
2 tablespoons butter
1 tablespoon sunflower oil
3 tablespoons white wine
6 tablespoons crème fraîche or heavy cream
2 tablespoons green peppercorns
salt and pepper
small bunch of fresh chives

1 Cut the salmon into strips and chop the unpeeled cucumber into large matchstick strips.

2 Melt the butter with the oil in a wok over moderate to high heat. Toss in the cucumber and stir-fry briefly. Add the salmon strips and stir-fry 2 or 3 minutes.

3 Add the wine and keep stir-frying a minute or two until it is almost all evaporated.

4 Reduce the heat and stir in the cream and green peppercorns. Season to taste, cook gently to heat through, and snip over the chives to serve.

CHICKEN BREAST STRIPS *with* BLOOD ORANGE *and* WALNUTS

under 15 minutes

If blood orange juice is not available, try red grapefruit juice or an orange and red fruit juice mixture.

1 pound skinless boneless chicken breasts
1 stalk of celery
$\frac{1}{2}$ cup walnuts
2 tablespoons butter
1 tablespoon oil
1 scallion
2 garlic cloves, minced
1 tablespoon red wine vinegar
$\frac{3}{4}$ cup blood orange juice
salt and pepper

1 Cut the chicken breasts into strips. Trim the celery and coarsely chop the walnuts.

2 Melt the butter with the oil in a wok over moderate to high heat. Snip in the scallion and celery. Add the garlic. Stir-fry 1 or 2 minutes.

3 Increase the heat to high and add the chicken strips. Stir-fry 3 or 4 minutes

4 Add the vinegar and stir-fry a minute or so, until it is almost all evaporated.

5 Stir in the orange juice with the chopped walnuts. Lower the heat and season to taste. Simmer gently 5 minutes.

DUCK BREAST STRIPS with CORN and HONEY

🌓 *under 20 minutes*

If you wish, you can trim the fat off before cutting the duck into strips.

1 pound skinless boneless duck breasts
1 tablespoon honey
2 teaspoons light soy sauce
small pinch of five-spice powder
1 tablespoon sherry vinegar
1 tablespoon oil
6 baby corn
salt and pepper

1 Cut the duck into strips.

2 In a bowl, mix the honey, soy sauce, five-spice powder, and half the vinegar. Stir in the duck strips so that they are well coated and let marinate at least 5 minutes.

3 Drain the duck, reserving the marinade. Heat the oil in the wok over high heat, tip in the drained duck strips, and stir-fry 2 or 3 minutes.

4 Lower the heat to moderate. Add the marinade and snip in the corn. Stir-fry a minute or two more.

5 Pour into a warmed serving dish. Deglaze the pan with the remaining vinegar, adjust the seasoning, and pour this over the duck.

Chicken Breast Strips with Blood Orange and Walnuts served on a bed of mixed salad leaves (see page 78)

● *FISH*

Buy fish which has been prepared as much as possible: whole fish should be cleaned and, if necessary, scaled; fillets should be skinned and steaks should be cut quite thinly. It is essential not to over-cook fish: broiling should be brief and poaching done at a very gentle simmer.

COD with TOMATO and WATERCRESS VINAIGRETTE

◗ *under 10 minutes*

Most poached or broiled firm white fish suit this vinaigrette.

1 scallion
½ bay leaf
small sprig of dried thyme
2 tablespoons white wine
4 or 5 sprigs of parsley
salt and pepper
4 cod steaks or skinned fillets, each weighing
    about 5 ounces
2 large ripe tomatoes
4 or 5 sprigs of watercress
1 tablespoon white wine vinegar
2 teaspoons Dijon-style mustard
⅓ cup olive oil

1 Snip the scallion into a large pan. Crumble in the bay leaf and the thyme. Add the white wine and snip in the stems from the parsley. Add just enough boiling water to be able to cover the cod and season well.

2 Bring back to a boil and simmer gently 1–2 minutes. Add the cod and poach gently about 5 minutes.

3 While the cod is poaching, make the vinaigrette: coarsely chop the tomatoes and whizz them in the food processor with most of the watercress, the vinegar, and mustard.

4 With the machine still running, dribble in the oil. Season to taste and whizz briefly to mix.

5 Drain the cod well and pour over the vinaigrette. Garnish with the reserved watercress.

TWO-CHEESE COD

◗ *under 15 minutes*

3 ounces sharp Cheddar cheese
2-ounce piece Parmesan cheese
1 tablespoon olive oil
1 tablespoon lemon juice
½ teaspoon mustard powder
pinch of grated nutmeg
salt and pepper
4 cod steaks or skinned fillets, each weighing
    about 5 ounces
pinch of cayenne

1 Heat the broiler. Slice the Cheddar thinly and grate the Parmesan.

2 Mix the oil with the lemon juice, mustard, and nutmeg. Season well and brush the cod with the mixture.

3 Broil the cod 1–2 minutes, then turn carefully and brush the tops again with the dressing. Broil this side a minute or so.

4 Cover the cod with slices of Cheddar and sprinkle generously with Parmesan. Season once more with pepper and broil until the cheeses are bubbling and slightly browned.

5 Sprinkle lightly with cayenne and pepper to serve.

Variation:
A number of cheeses will work in place of the Cheddar: try a good strong Gloucester, or Red Leicester or a blue cheese.

SOLE with ORANGE and LEMON BUTTER

🕐 *under 10 minutes*

4 large skinned sole or flounder fillets
salt and pepper
4 tablespoons butter
½ orange
½ lemon

1 Heat the broiler.

2 Season the fish with salt and pepper. Dice the butter. Peel off a few thin strips of zest from the orange and the lemon. Cut the fruit halves in half again and reserve one piece of each to serve. Squeeze the juice from the others and mix.

3 Whizz the pared zest in the food processor until finely chopped. Add two-thirds of the butter and half the juice and season to taste. Whizz again briefly until well blended.

4 Brush some of the mixture over the tops of the fish fillets and broil 2 or 3 minutes. Turn the fish carefully, spread some more of the flavored butter over the fish, and broil a minute or two more.

5 Deglaze the broiler pan with the remaining juice and butter.

6 Season this sauce if necessary, pour it over the fish, and serve with the remaining lemon and orange quarters cut into wedges.

Sole with Orange and Lemon Butter

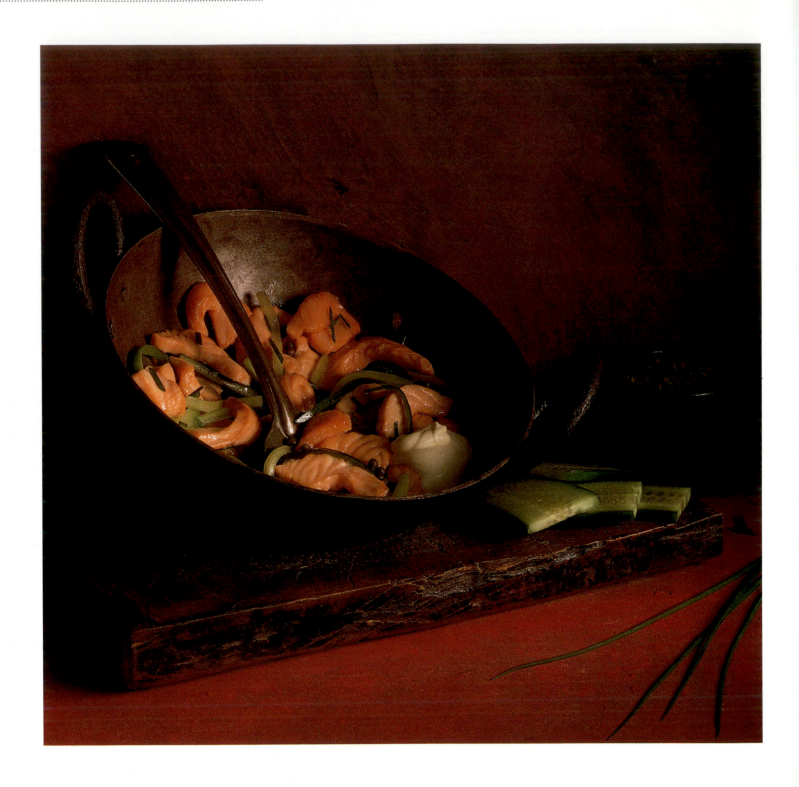

SALMON SLICES with MUSHROOM and PARSLEY CRUST

🕐 *under 15 minutes*

This dish works very well accompanied by the creamed mushrooms as served on English muffins on page 34.

2 ounces mushrooms
2 tablespoons oil
1 tablespoon lemon juice
1 tablespoon whole-grain mustard
2 tablespoons dry bread crumbs
1 scallion
3 or 4 sprigs of parsley
salt and pepper
4 salmon scaloppine (thin slices of fillet), each
   weighing about 5 ounces

1 Heat the broiler. Finely chop the mushrooms.

2 In a bowl, mix the oil, lemon juice, mustard, mushrooms, and bread crumbs. Snip in the scallion and most of the parsley, season generously, and mix in well.

3 Broil the salmon slices, skin side up, 1 or 2 minutes. Turn them over, spread the mushroom mixture over them, and pat it into the flesh. Broil until the crust is firm and the fish is cooked to taste.

4 Let rest about 1 minute and then snip over the remaining parsley to serve.

Salmon Strips with Cucumber and Crème Fraîche (page 47)

SALMON STEAKS with a LIGHT SALSA

🕐 *under 15 minutes*

If you don't have any chili peppers, just add some cayenne or Tabasco sauce to taste.

1 small fresh chili pepper
$\frac{1}{4}$ pound ripe tomatoes
$\frac{1}{2}$ lime
2 garlic cloves
2 tablespoon olive oil
salt and pepper
4 salmon steaks
3 scallions
3 or 4 sprigs cilantro
pinch of sugar

1 Heat the broiler. Halve the chili and remove its seeds. Chop the tomatoes into small pieces, squeeze the juice of the lime, and mince the garlic.

2 In a bowl, mix half the lime juice with half the oil. Season with pepper and brush this mixture over both sides of the salmon steaks.

3 Broil the steaks a few minutes on each side, until cooked to taste.

4 Meanwhile, heat the remaining oil in a sauté pan over moderate heat. Snip in the scallions and chili and add the garlic. Cook 2 or 3 minutes, stirring frequently.

5 Stir in the tomatoes, almost all the cilantro, and the remaining lime juice. Season to taste with salt, pepper, and sugar. Cook 2 or 3 minutes until the tomatoes are just softened.

6 Spoon a little of the salsa on each of 4 warmed plates, place a salmon steak on each, and snip over the remaining cilantro.

PAN-FRIED TROUT with NUT SAUCE

🕐 *under 20 minutes*

4 small rainbow trout, cleaned
2 garlic cloves
2 tablespoons flour
4 tablespoons butter
2 tablespoons oil
3 tablespoons white wine
1 lemon
$\frac{3}{4}$ cup slivered almonds
salt and pepper
2 or 3 small sprigs of parsley

1 Season the fish well inside and out. Mince the garlic cloves and divide one of them among the insides of each fish. Sprinkle the fish lightly with flour.

2 Melt half the butter with half the oil in a large skillet over high heat and brown the trout on both sides.

3 Turn the heat down and add the white wine and the juice from the lemon. Cover and simmer about 10 minutes, turning once.

4 While the fish are cooking, in a separate pan melt the remaining butter with the remaining oil over moderate heat. Add the remaining garlic and cook a minute or two. Add the nuts and sauté them, stirring frequently, until they are well browned.

5 When the fish are cooked, transfer them to warmed plates. Boil the liquid in the pan until only about 1 tablespoon is left. Then add the nut and garlic mixture to the pan and mix well.

6 Season the nut sauce, if necessary, pour it over the fish, and snip over the parsley to serve.

POULTRY

*Use free-range chicken for a better flavor. Thighs
and drumsticks take longer to cook but have more
taste than breast meat, so it is a good idea to use
them in combination whenever possible. Chicken
breasts are best cooked in a moist sauce to keep
them from drying out.*

QUICK POULE au POT with SMOKED HAM

🌓   *under 20 minutes*

2 skinless boneless chicken thighs
2 skinless boneless chicken breast halves
1 onion
2 garlic cloves
2 stalks of celery
2 bay leaves
pinch of dried thyme
6 whole black peppercorns
salt and pepper
2 or 3 sprigs of flat-leaf parsley
$\frac{1}{4}$ pound baby carrots
$\frac{1}{4}$ pound baby turnips
4 baby leeks
2 thick slices of cooked ham
2 tablespoons capers
3 gherkin pickles
$\frac{3}{4}$ cup mayonnaise

1 Cut the chicken thighs and breasts in half
lengthwise. Halve the onion and garlic cloves.
Coarsely chop the celery.

2 Put enough hot water to cover the chicken in a
large pan with the onion, crumbled bay leaves,
celery, garlic, thyme, peppercorns, salt, and the
stems from the parsley. Bring to a boil and simmer
gently a minute or two.

3 Add the chicken pieces and surround them
with the carrots, turnips, and leeks. Arrange the
slices of ham over the top of the chicken pieces.

4 Bring back to a boil. Cover and simmer gently
about 10 minutes.

5 While the chicken is cooking, briefly whizz the
parsley, capers, and gherkins together in the food
processor until coarsely chopped. Do not over-
process. Add the mayonnaise and pepper to taste
and whizz very briefly to mix well.

6 At the end of the cooking time, take out the
ham and let cool slightly.

7 Transfer the chicken pieces and vegetables to a
warmed serving dish with 3 or 4 tablespoons of
the cooking liquid.

8 Dice the ham, discarding any fat, and stir into
the sauce with another 2 tablespoons of the
cooking liquid. Serve this separately in a bowl.

BROILED CHICKEN with DEVILED RED FRUIT SAUCE

🌑   *under 20 minutes*

Speed the cooking by cutting the chicken thighs in
half lengthwise.

8 small boneless chicken thighs
salt and pepper
2 tablespoons oil
$\frac{1}{2}$ cup mixed red fruit preserves
$\frac{1}{2}$ teaspoon Worcestershire sauce
pinch of ground ginger
1 tablespoon Dijon-style mustard
3 or 4 drops of Tabasco sauce
3 tablespoons crème fraîche or heavy cream

1 Season the chicken thighs with salt and pepper.

2 Heat the oil in a large skillet over moderate to
high heat. Cook the chicken thighs 2–3 minutes
on each side, until well browned.

3 Reduce the heat and add all the remaining
ingredients, except the cream. Mix well, cover, and
simmer about 10 minutes, turning the chicken
halfway through.

4 Transfer the chicken to warmed plates and
adjust the seasoning of the sauce.

5 Lightly fold the cream into the sauce so that it
is streaked red and white. Heat through briefly and
then spoon around the chicken.

CHICKEN DRUMSTICKS with SALSA VERDE

🕐 *under 20 minutes*

4 anchovy fillets in oil
½ lemon
4 or 5 sprigs of flat-leaf parsley
2 garlic cloves
1½ tablespoons capers
1 tablespoon brown sugar
¼ cup oil
pinch of cayenne
salt and pepper
8 small chicken drumsticks

1   Heat the broiler. Drain, pat dry, and coarsely chop the anchovy fillets. Grate the zest from the lemon and squeeze its juice.

2   Put the anchovies in the food processor with the lemon zest, parsley, peeled garlic, capers, sugar, 1 tablespoon of the oil, the cayenne, and salt and pepper. Whizz until smooth.

3   Spread the chicken drumsticks with a little of the mixture and broil about 10–15 minutes, turning 3 or 4 times to ensure even cooking.

4   When the drumsticks are nearly cooked, heat the remaining oil in a sauté pan over moderate heat and cook the remaining sauce mixture 2 or 3 minutes, stirring frequently.

5   Add the lemon juice and the remaining oil and adjust the seasoning if necessary.

6   Pour any juices from the broiler pan into the sauce before serving.

CHICKEN in GOAT CHEESE and CHIVE SAUCE

🕐 *under 15 minutes*

Use a piece of goat cheese in log form. Cut off the rind before adding it to the sauce.

4 skinless boneless chicken breast halves
2 tablespoons oil
1 tablespoon Dijon-style mustard
pepper
2 tablespoons butter
3 ounces soft goat cheese
½ cup crème fraîche or heavy cream
pinch of celery salt
pinch of cayenne
bunch of fresh chives

1   Cut the chicken breast halves in half lengthwise. Mix half the oil with the mustard and some pepper and brush this mixture over the chicken.

2   In a large sauté pan, melt the butter with the remaining oil over moderate to high heat. Brown the chicken pieces 2 or 3 minutes on each side and remove them from the pan.

3   Crumble in the goat cheese and heat until completely melted. Stir in the cream. Season to taste with celery salt, pepper, and cayenne.

4   Return the chicken to the pan and simmer gently about 5 minutes.

5   Snip over the chives to serve.

STIR-FRIED CHICKEN, OYSTER MUSHROOMS, and SCALLIONS

🕐 *under 15 minutes*

4 skinless boneless chicken breast halves
1 teaspoon soy sauce
1 lemon
salt and pepper
1 teaspoon sesame oil
1 tablespoon sunflower oil
4 scallions
1 garlic clove
3 ounces oyster mushrooms

1   Cut the chicken in large dice and toss in a bowl with the soy sauce, the juice from half the lemon, and some pepper.

2   Heat the oils in a wok over moderate to high heat. Snip in the scallions. Mince the garlic and add it. Stir-fry 1 or 2 minutes.

3   Drain the chicken, reserving the liquid. Stir-fry the chicken pieces 2 or 3 minutes.

4   Add the reserved liquid and stir-fry a minute or so more until most of the liquid has evaporated.

5   Tear or snip in the mushrooms and stir-fry 2 or 3 minutes more.

6   Adjust the seasoning, if necessary, sprinkle over the remaining lemon juice, and stir-fry briefly, then serve.

Variation:
Dribble the sesame oil over the dish as a dressing at the end instead of using it in the cooking.

CHICKEN in SWEET WHITE WINE

🕐 *under 20 minutes*

2 skinless boneless chicken breast halves
2 skinless boneless chicken thighs
2 tablespoons flour
pinch of celery salt
small pinch of dried sage
salt and pepper
2 garlic cloves
2 tablespoons butter
1 tablespoon oil
2 scallions
$\frac{3}{4}$ cup sweet white wine
2 tablespoons crème fraîche or heavy cream

1 Cut the chicken breast halves and thighs in half lengthwise. Season the flour with celery salt, sage, and pepper and dust the chicken pieces with it. Mince the garlic.

2 Melt the butter with the oil in a large skillet over moderate heat, snip in the scallions, and add the garlic. Sauté 2 or 3 minutes, stirring frequently.

3 Add the chicken pieces and pour in the wine. Cover and cook about 8–10 minutes, turning the chicken pieces over halfway through.

4 Transfer the chicken to warmed plates. Boil the liquid in the pan to reduce it a little if necessary.

5 Stir in the cream, season to taste, and pour over the chicken to serve.

Variation:
Add a few seedless grapes or raisins to the sauce with the cream.

CHICKEN BREASTS in COCONUT MILK with MANGO

🕐 *under 25 minutes*

4 skinless boneless chicken breast halves
1 lime
salt and pepper
1 not-too-ripe mango
$\frac{1}{2}$ cup thick coconut milk
1 tablespoon sunflower oil
2 scallions
pinch of ground ginger or cayenne

1 Cut each breast half in half lengthwise and season with the juice from the lime and pepper. Peel and slice the mango flesh, reserving all the juice.

2 Mix 1 tablespoon of the coconut milk with the sunflower oil and heat this in a large skillet over moderate heat. Snip in the scallions and sauté them 1 or 2 minutes, stirring frequently.

3 Add the chicken pieces and cook them about 2 minutes on each side.

4 Add the remaining coconut milk and lime juice with the mango slices and juices. Cover the pan and simmer gently 8 minutes, turning the chicken halfway through.

5 Transfer the chicken and mango pieces to warmed plates. Boil the sauce a little to reduce it slightly. Adjust the seasoning with salt and pepper if necessary, pour over the chicken, and serve with a little ginger or cayenne sprinkled over the top.

Variation:
Crush in some pink peppercorns before boiling the sauce for even more color and flavor.

DUCK BREASTS with BLACK CURRANT SAUCE

🕐 *under 15 minutes*

4 boneless duck breast halves
$\frac{1}{2}$ cup black currant or blueberry preserves
$\frac{1}{4}$ cup red wine
1 tablespoon green peppercorns
bunch of watercress
salt and pepper

1 Heat the broiler.

2 Cut several deep diagonal incisions through the fat and into the flesh along the length of each breast half. Season them with pepper.

3 Broil the duck 5 minutes with the fat side uppermost, until the fat is crisp and deep golden. Turn them over and broil another 5 minutes.

4 Meanwhile in a small pan, heat the black currant preserves with the wine and green peppercorns. Season to taste and simmer gently until the duck is ready.

5 Put the duck on warmed plates and surround with sprigs of watercress.

6 Stir any juices from the broiler pan into the sauce before serving separately.

Chicken Breasts in Coconut Milk with Mango

● BEEF and VEAL

The best and most tender filet mignon or sirloin steaks are expensive, but cook very rapidly and there is no waste as they are well trimmed.

BASIC BROILED STEAK

🕐 *under 10 minutes*

Try to ensure that the steaks are at room temperature before cooking. If they come straight from the refrigerator they will shrink under the heat and will not cook satisfactorily in the short time involved. The broiler must be very hot and the steaks should be as near the heat as possible so that the outsides seal quickly to keep in the juices. Turn the steaks with tongs or a spatula to avoid piercing them.

4 filet mignon or boneless sirloin steaks, each
   weighing about 5 ounces and about $\frac{3}{4}$ inch thick
1 tablespoon oil
pepper

1 Heat the broiler until it is very hot.

2 Brush the steaks on both sides with the oil and then season generously with pepper only.

3 Broil 2 to 5 minutes on each side, depending on how well done you want the steaks to be.

4 Serve topped with a pat of one of the savory butters here.

● SAVORY BUTTERS

These are easier to make if the butter is slightly soft. Use unsalted butter as it is then easier to adjust the seasoning. Put the butter mixtures on small squares of foil, roll them into a cylinder, and freeze while the steaks are cooking. This may then be easily diced or sliced across into neat disks to place on the cooked steak.

If your food processor only has a large bowl, double the quantities and freeze the extra.

OLIVE and ANCHOVY BUTTER

🕐 *under 5 minutes*

4 tablespoons butter
wedge of lemon
4 anchovy fillets in oil
$\frac{1}{3}$ cup pitted black olives
pepper

1 Dice the butter and coarsely chop the lemon wedge.

2 Drain, rinse, and pat dry the anchovies. Snip them into the food processor and whizz with the lemon and olives until smooth.

3 Add the butter with pepper to taste and whizz again briefly until well mixed.

GARLIC and PARSLEY BUTTER

🕐 *under 5 minutes*

4 tablespoons butter
2 garlic cloves
2 or 3 sprigs of flat-leaf parsley
salt and pepper

1 Dice the butter.

2 In a food processor, whizz the butter with the peeled garlic, parsley, and seasoning to taste until smooth.

MUSTARD BUTTER

🕐 *under 5 minutes*

4 tablespoons butter
1 tablespoon whole-grain mustard
1 tablespoon Dijon-style mustard
1 tablespoon lemon juice
pepper

1 Dice the butter.

2 In a food processor, whizz the butter with the mustards, lemon juice, and pepper to taste until smooth.

BLUE CHEESE BUTTER

🕐 *under 5 minutes*

4 tablespoons butter
3 ounces blue cheese
1 tablespoon port
6 whole black peppercorns

1 Dice the butter.

2 In a food processor, whizz the cheese with the port and peppercorns until fairly smooth.

3 Add the butter and whizz again briefly until well mixed.

VEAL SCALOPPINE with LEMON and SAGE BUTTER

🕐 *under 10 minutes*

To dust small items with flour quickly, use a small strainer.

2 tablespoons flour
salt and pepper
4 thinly beaten veal scaloppine, each weighing
   about 3 ounces
1 lemon
4 tablespoons butter
1 tablespoon oil
2 or 3 fresh sage leaves

1   Season the flour with salt and pepper. Dust the scaloppine lightly with the flour. Squeeze the juice from the lemon.

2   Melt the butter with the oil in a large skillet over moderate heat. Snip in the sage leaves and cook 1 or 2 minutes.

3   Add the veal scaloppine and cook 2 minutes on each side.

4   Add half the lemon juice and seasoning to taste. Cook 1 more minute over very high heat, turning the veal halfway through.

5   Put the veal scaloppine on warmed plates and deglaze the pan with the remaining lemon juice. Adjust the seasoning if necessary and pour over the veal to serve.

Calves' Liver with Lime

BEEF with MUSHROOM SAUCE

🕐 *under 15 minutes*

A more economical version of this dish may be made using minute steak.

12 black peppercorns
4 pieces of boneless sirloin steak
$\frac{1}{2}$ pound mushrooms
1 garlic clove
4 tablespoons butter
2 tablespoons oil
2 scallions
1 tablespoon cognac
$\frac{3}{4}$ cup light cream
salt and pepper
small bunch of fresh chives

1   In the food processor coarsely crush the whole peppercorns and press them into the steaks. Slice the mushrooms thinly and mince the garlic.

2   Melt the butter with the oil in a large sauté pan over moderate heat. Snip in the scallions and add the garlic. Sauté a minute or two, stirring frequently.

3   Increase the heat to high and sear the steaks a minute or two on each side. Remove the steaks and keep them warm.

4   Reduce the heat again to moderate and add the mushrooms and cognac. Sauté 2 or 3 minutes.

5   Stir in the cream, adjust the seasoning if necessary, and return the steaks to the pan, along with any juices. Simmer gently a few minutes, depending on how well done you want the steaks to be.

6   Snip the chives over to serve.

CALVES' LIVER with LIME

🕐 *under 10 minutes*

The liver should be sliced paper-thin for best results. You may have to fry the slices one or two at a time. Liver is at its best if only cooked very briefly and still moist and pink inside. Increase the cooking times if you prefer liver well done, but be very careful as it quickly becomes tough if over-cooked.

1 lime
2 tablespoons butter
1 tablespoon oil
3 scallions
1 tablespoon sherry vinegar
2 tablespoons sweet vermouth
salt and pepper
1 pound very thin slices of calves' liver

1   Zest the lime and squeeze its juice.

2   Melt the butter with the oil in a wok over moderate to high heat. Snip in the scallions and add the lime zest. Stir-fry 1 or 2 minutes.

3   Add the sherry vinegar and vermouth with seasoning to taste and stir-fry until only about 1 tablespoon of liquid is left.

4   Turn up the heat to high and add the liver. Fry 1 or 2 minutes only on each side. Tip out into a warmed serving dish.

5   Deglaze the pan with the lime juice, adjust the seasoning, and pour this over the liver to serve.

LAMB

The better cuts of good quality lamb, including the small tender chops cut from the rib and thin noisettes, cook quite quickly. The cooking times given are for slightly pink lamb. Add a few minutes more if you prefer your lamb well done. Make sure that the pieces of lamb are well trimmed of fat.

LAMB CHOPS with APRICOT, CUMIN, and GARLIC SAUCE

🕐 *under 25 minutes*

4 dried apricots
$\frac{1}{2}$ cup white wine
8 small lamb chops
salt and pepper
$\frac{1}{2}$ teaspoon ground cumin
$\frac{1}{2}$ teaspoon lemon
2 garlic cloves
1 tablespoon oil
2 scallions
1 tablespoon honey

1 Coarsely chop the apricots and put them in a small pan with the wine. Bring to a boil and simmer 2 or 3 minutes.

2 Season the lamb chops with pepper and cumin. Finely grate the zest from the lemon and squeeze its juice. Mince the garlic. Drain the apricots and reserve the wine.

3 Heat the oil in a large skillet over moderate heat. Add the garlic and lemon zest. Snip in the scallions and apricots.

4 Sauté 2 or 3 minutes, stirring frequently.

5 Turn up the heat slightly and cook the lamb chops 3–5 minutes on each side, depending on how well you wish them to be cooked.

6 Transfer the lamb to a warmed serving dish and keep warm.

7 Deglaze the pan with the honey, lemon juice, and reserved wine. Stir and boil a minute or two to reduce to a coating consistency. Adjust the seasoning and pour this sauce over the lamb to serve.

NOISETTES in an ALMOND and LEMON CRUST

🕐 *under 15 minutes*

This treatment works equally well with broiled noisettes and broiled or fried lamb chops.

$\frac{1}{2}$ lemon
2 tablespoons olive oil
$\frac{3}{4}$ cup sliced almonds
pinch of ground mace
salt and pepper
8 small lamb noisettes (boned loin chops), each
   weighing about 2–$2\frac{1}{2}$ ounces
$1\frac{1}{2}$ tablespoons butter

1 Halve the lemon half and chop one quarter coarsely. Squeeze the juice from the other piece.

2 In the food processor, whizz to a paste the chopped lemon with half the oil, two-thirds of the almonds, the mace, and seasoning to taste. Spread the noisettes with this mixture.

3 Heat the remaining oil in a large skillet over moderate to high heat and cook the noisettes in it 3–5 minutes on each side, depending on how well done you want the lamb to be.

4 After the noisettes have been carefully turned, add the butter with the remaining almonds to the pan and sauté them as the lamb continues to cook, stirring them frequently.

5 Put the cooked noisettes on warmed plates. Deglaze the pan with the lemon juice and adjust the seasoning if necessary. Pour the sautéed almonds and pan juices over the lamb to serve.

PAN-FRIED LAMB CHOPS with BABY VEGETABLES

◑ *under 20 minutes*

8 small lamb chops
salt and pepper
$\frac{1}{2}$ pound ripe tomatoes
1 garlic clove
1 head baby romaine lettuce
2 tablespoons oil
2 scallions
$\frac{1}{4}$ pound baby carrots
$\frac{1}{4}$ pound green beans
$\frac{1}{4}$ pound frozen petite peas
pinch of sugar

1 Season the lamb chops with pepper. Chop the tomatoes, mince the garlic, and shred the lettuce.

2 Heat the oil in a large skillet over a moderate heat. Snip in the scallions and add the garlic. Cook 1 or 2 minutes, stirring frequently.

3 Increase the heat slightly and add the lamb chops. Cook 3–5 minutes on each side, depending on how well done you want the lamb to be.

4 Transfer the lamb to a serving dish and keep warm.

5 Lower the heat to moderate. Add the carrots to the pan and sauté them 2 or 3 minutes.

6 Add the green beans and sauté a minute or two more. Add the tomatoes, lettuce, and peas with a pinch of sugar, cover, and simmer 2 or 3 minutes.

7 Adjust the seasoning, if necessary, and pour over the lamb to serve.

● PORK and HAM

Pork must be thoroughly cooked, but it is quite easy to overcook it so that it becomes tough and dry. Cooking it in a tightly covered pan helps the meat retain its succulence. Buy trimmed pork chops and flatten them slightly with a meat pounder or rolling pin to speed cooking.

HAM STEAKS with DEVILED CUMBERLAND SAUCE

◑ *under 20 minutes*

4 ham steaks, each about $\frac{3}{4}$ inch thick
salt and pepper
$\frac{1}{2}$ orange
wedge of lemon
2 shallots
$\frac{1}{2}$ cup red currant jelly
2 tablespoons port
1 teaspoon arrowroot
1 teaspoon Worcestershire sauce
1 teaspoon mustard powder
1 teaspoon red wine vinegar
pinch of cayenne
2 tablespoons oil

1 Season the ham steaks with pepper.

2 Pare off several strips of zest from the orange and lemon. Coarsely chop the shallots. Whizz them in the food processor with the pared zest until puréed. Squeeze in the juice from the orange and lemon and add all the remaining ingredients except the oil. Whizz again until well mixed.

3 Heat the oil in a large skillet over moderate heat and add the sauce mixture. Sauté 2 or 3 minutes, stirring frequently.

4 Remove all but 2 tablespoons of the liquid from the pan and keep warm. Increase the heat slightly and add the ham steaks. Cook about 4 minutes on each side.

5 Return the rest of the sauce to the pan. Cover and simmer gently about 3–5 minutes. Adjust the seasoning, if necessary, to serve.

"WILD" PORK CHOPS with BEER and JUNIPER BERRIES

 under 25 minutes

8 juniper berries
2 garlic cloves
pinch of dried thyme
salt and pepper
2 tablespoons oil
4 thin pork loin chops
$\frac{1}{2}$ pound ripe tomatoes
2 scallions
$\frac{1}{2}$ cup light beer

1   In the food processor, whizz the juniper berries with one of the garlic cloves, the thyme, some pepper, and half the oil. Spread the chops with this mixture. Coarsely chop the tomatoes and mince the other garlic clove.

2   Heat the remaining oil in a skillet over high heat and brown the chops 3 or 4 minutes on each side. Transfer them to a warmed dish and keep warm.

3   Reduce the heat to moderate and snip in the scallions. Add the minced garlic and the tomatoes with any remaining juniper berry mixture. Sauté 2 or 3 minutes, stirring frequently.

4   Add the beer and boil a minute or two.

5   Return the chops to the pan. Cover, and simmer gently about 7 minutes. Adjust the seasoning to serve.

Variation:
Shred some cabbage into this dish after the chops have been returned to the pan.

PORK CHOPS with APPLE and CALVADOS SAUCE

under 25 minutes

If the chops are really small, you may need 2 per person.

4 thin pork loin chops
3 firm red-skinned apples
3 scallions
1 garlic clove
2 tablespoons oil
2 tablespoons apple juice
salt and pepper
2 tablespoons calvados or brandy

1   Season the pork chops. Halve and core the apples. Coarsely chop 2 of them and cut the third into thick slices.

2   Put the chopped apples in the food processor, snip in the scallions and add the peeled garlic. Pour in half the oil and the apple juice. Season with salt and pepper and whizz until well blended.

3   In a large skillet, heat the remaining oil over moderate heat. Add the apple mixture and sliced apples and sauté 1 or 2 minutes, stirring frequently.

4   Remove all but about 2 tablespoons of the mixture from the pan, turn up the heat slightly, and add the chops. Cover and cook about 10–12 minutes, turning the chops halfway through, until the juices run quite clear when they are pierced.

5   Return the remaining mixture to the pan and add the calvados. Simmer gently 1 or 2 minutes then adjust the seasoning, if necessary.

Pork Chops with Apple and Calvados Sauce

5

VEGETABLES and SALADS

When cooking in a hurry there is little time to devote to fussy accompaniments. Moreover, good fresh vegetables require the minimum of cooking to preserve their flavor and texture. For this reason we favor techniques like broiling and stir-frying. We also often cook our vegetables either in combination or along with potatoes, rice, or noodles.

We take advantage of the increasing number of quick-cook varieties of rice now available. We are also particularly fond of those types of Chinese noodles which need only to be soaked in hot water to be ready to eat. They come in an interesting variety of flavors and are good stir-fried with flavorings and other vegetables.

Top: Grilled Mediterranean Vegetables (page 73); bottom: Basmati Rice with Pine Nuts and Raisins (page 68)

BASMATI RICE with PINE NUTS and RAISINS

🕐 *under 15 minutes*

You can now buy varieties of basmati rice that cook in 10 minutes.

2 cups chicken or vegetable stock or water
$1\frac{1}{3}$ cups basmati or other long-grain rice
4 tablespoons butter
2 tablespoon oil
$\frac{1}{3}$ cup golden raisins
salt and pepper
2 or 3 sprigs of cilantro
$\frac{2}{3}$ cup pine nuts

1 Bring the stock or water to a boil.

2 Rinse the rice thoroughly in a strainer under cold running water. Let it drain.

3 Melt the butter with the oil in a large heavy saucepan over a moderate heat.

4 Add the rice and raisins. Stir well to ensure that all the rice grains are coated.

5 Pour in the boiling stock or water, add a generous pinch of salt, stir, and bring back to a boil.

6 Cover the pan and simmer gently 8–10 minutes, until all the stock or water has been absorbed and the rice is tender.

7 Snip over the coriander, stir in the pine nuts, and season to taste.

Variations:

1 For extra flavor, sauté 2 or 3 snipped scallions in the butter and oil before adding the rice and then add a pinch of ground cinnamon with the raisins.

2 Alternatively, add $\frac{3}{4}$ cup frozen petite peas with the rice at the beginning of cooking and stir in $\frac{1}{3}$ cup toasted cashews at the end.

TWICE-COOKED NOODLES with BABY CORN

🕐 *under 15 minutes*

3 tablespoons olive oil
1 pound egg noodles
3 scallions
6 baby corn
salt and pepper

1 Put $4\frac{1}{2}$ quarts of water in a large pot over high heat. Alternatively, to speed things up, heat most of the water in the pan and the rest in the microwave. Add a generous pinch of salt and 1 tablespoon of the oil to the water in the pan.

2 Add the noodles and cook them 3–4 minutes until just soft but still with some resistance to the bite. Drain well.

3 While the noodles are cooking, heat the remaining oil in a wok over moderate heat. Snip in the scallions and corn. Stir-fry 2 or 3 minutes.

4 Add the cooked and drained noodles with seasoning to taste and stir-fry another minute or so.

Variations:

1 To accompany highly flavored dishes, serve the noodles plainly cooked with 1 tablespoon of oil stirred into them.

2 If you use Chinese cellophane noodles, they need only be soaked in boiling water before stir-frying.

3 Stir-fry the noodles with 2 ounces snipped snow peas and a snipped seeded chili pepper.

SAUTÉED ZUCCHINI SHREDS

🕐 *under 10 minutes*

Do not peel the zucchini for this dish. Their size is not important as the shreds cook so quickly, but smaller zucchini will be sweeter.

½ pound zucchini
4 tablespoons butter
1 tablespoon sunflower oil
salt and pepper

1 Finely shred the zucchini in the food processor, using the shredding blade.

2 Melt the butter with the oil in a large sauté pan over moderate to high heat.

3 Season the butter very generously with salt and pepper.

4 When the pan is very hot, tip in the zucchini shreds and stir-fry them briefly until just softened and well coated with the seasoned butter and oil.

Variations:

1 For even more flavor, snip in some fresh tarragon, or add some minced garlic to the pan and cook for a minute or so before adding the zucchini.

2 Sprinkle the shreds with some lemon juice just before serving.

GREEN BEANS with ANCHOVY BEURRE BLANC SAUCE

🕐 *under 15 minutes*

It is essential to use unsalted butter for this sauce as the anchovies are so salty. To trim green beans in a hurry: bang a handful down on one end to align them and then cut those ends off, then repeat with the other end.

1 pound fine green beans
3 canned anchovies in oil
2 shallots
¾ cup white wine
1 stick unsalted butter
salt and pepper

1 Trim the green beans.

2 Put the beans in a large pan, cover with boiling water, and add a generous pinch of salt.

3 Bring to a boil and simmer 3–5 minutes, until the beans are just tender but still firm to the bite. Drain well.

4 While the beans are cooking, make the sauce. Drain and pat the anchovies dry. In the food processor, whizz the shallots and anchovies to a coarse paste.

5 Put this mixture in a small saucepan with the wine, bring to a boil, and simmer a few minutes until syrupy.

6 Off the heat, add the butter in small pieces, whisking them in one at a time until the sauce is smooth and shiny. Season with pepper.

7 Toss the drained beans in the sauce to serve.

STIR-FRIED LEEKS with JUNIPER BERRIES

🕐 *under 20 minutes*

This dish goes well with broiled meat. Try to use baby leeks if possible. Older leeks will have to be simmered longer.

6 leeks
1 tablespoon juniper berries
1 garlic clove
4 tablespoons butter
1 tablespoon olive oil
2 tablespoons white wine
1 tablespoon lemon juice
salt and pepper

1   Trim the leeks and halve them. Wash out the grit carefully under cold running water. Pat the leeks dry and snip them into fine slices. Lightly crush the juniper berries and mince the garlic clove.

2   Melt the butter with the oil in a sauté pan over moderate heat and add the juniper berries and garlic. Stir-fry a minute or so.

3   Add the leeks and stir-fry 2 or 3 minutes.

4   Add the white wine and lemon juice. Cover the pan and simmer gently about 3 minutes.

5   Season well with salt and pepper.

Variation:
Stir in 3 or 4 tablespoons of cream and a small pinch of grated nutmeg to serve with poultry or eggs.

BUTTERED BABY CARROTS with VERMOUTH

🕐 *under 15 minutes*

You can use older carrots, but they must be scraped and sliced and cooked a few minutes longer.

1 pound baby carrots
4 tablespoons butter
2 tablespoons sweet vermouth
salt and pepper

1   Put the carrots in a large pan and add just enough water to cover. Add a generous pinch of salt and bring to a boil over high heat.

2   Lower the heat and simmer gently 4–6 minutes until the carrots are just tender but still firm. Drain well.

3   Return the carrots to the rinsed-out pan and add the butter and vermouth. Season well with salt and pepper.

4   Toss the contents of the pan over high heat until the carrots are evenly coated with the mixture and have browned slightly.

Left: Stir-fried Leeks with Juniper Berries; right: Buttered Baby Carrots with Vermouth

STIR-FRIED SCALLIONS *with* FIVE-SPICE POWDER

◖ *under 10 minutes*

Use the scallions in their entirety, including the green tops.

$\frac{1}{2}$ pound scallions
2 tablespoons sunflower oil
$\frac{1}{2}$ teaspoon five-spice powder
1 teaspoon sesame oil
1 tablespoon lemon juice
salt and pepper
soy sauce (optional)

1 Snip the scallions into 2-inch lengths.

2 Heat the sunflower oil with the five-spice powder in a wok over high heat.

3 Add the scallions and stir-fry them 4 or 5 minutes, until tender but still crunchy.

4 Dress with the sesame oil and lemon juice. Season with salt and pepper or soy sauce to serve.

BABY NEW POTATOES *with* FRESH HERBS

◖ *under 15 minutes*

The smaller the potatoes are the faster they cook; if you can't get really small ones, cut them in half. Use any of the suggested herbs, either on their own or in combination.

1 pound baby new potatoes
4 tablespoons butter
4 or 5 sprigs of fresh herbs, such as chives, parsley, mint, or basil
salt and pepper

1 Scrub the potatoes but do not peel them.

2 Put the potatoes in a large pan, cover with boiling water, and add a generous pinch of salt. Bring the water back to a boil, reduce the heat, and simmer 4–6 minutes, until the potatoes are just tender but still firm. Drain well.

3 Return the potatoes to the rinsed-out pan, add the butter, and snip in the herbs. Season well with salt and pepper.

4 Toss the potatoes over high heat until they are all well coated with the herbs and butter.

Variations:
1 Dress the cooked potatoes with some Orange and Lemon Butter (see page 51).

2 Instead of butter, stir in $\frac{3}{4}$ cup thick plain yogurt, crème fraîche, or sour cream and snip in some fresh dill leaves. This dish also works very well cold for buffets or picnics.

GRILLED MEDITERRANEAN VEGETABLES

🕐 *under 15 minutes*

2 small fennel bulbs
2 red bell peppers
2 yellow bell peppers
4 baby zucchini
2 red onions
4 plum tomatoes
¼ cup olive oil
salt

1 Heat the broiler.

2 Cut the vegetables in half lengthwise. Take out the woody core from the fennel bulbs. Remove the seeds and pith from the bell peppers.

3 Put the vegetables on the broiler rack and brush them well with oil. Sprinkle with coarse salt.

4 Broil the vegetables, turning as necessary and basting with more oil, until they are well browned all over, 6–10 minutes.

Variations:

1 Use oil flavored with herbs, spices, or chili.

2 Snip some fresh oregano or thyme over the vegetables before serving.

GREEN PEAS with LETTUCE and SCALLIONS

🕐 *under 10 minutes*

Frozen petite peas are picked and processed so rapidly that they are more sweet, tender, and flavorful than all but the green peas from your own garden. Use them straight from the package and don't bother thawing them first.

4 tablespoons butter
2 heads baby romaine lettuce
4 scallions
1 or 2 sprigs of fresh summer savory
3 cups frozen petite peas
pinch of sugar
salt and pepper

1 Melt the butter in a heavy pan over moderate heat.

2 Shred the lettuce coarsely into the pan. Snip in the scallions and herbs. Add the peas with the sugar, about 2 tablespoons of water, and salt and pepper to taste.

3 Cover the pan tightly, bring to a boil, and simmer very gently until just tender, 5–7 minutes depending on the size of the peas. Shake the pan once or twice during cooking.

Variations:

1 Use fresh thyme or mint instead of the savory.

2 Instead of using butter, first snip 2 slices of bacon into the pan and fry them until crisp, then add the other ingredients.

● SALADS

More than just the quickest and most satisfying form of vegetable accompaniment, salads can make exciting first courses, healthy snack meals, and substantial main courses.

Our approach to making a good salad is simple: freshness and variety are all. Choose from our checklists of good ingredients to make new and interesting combinations every time. We have arranged them so that those ingredients that broadly line up across the page will marry well to give a good salad. Whatever your mix, however, as long as you ensure a good balance of colors, textures, and tastes the results will be rewarding.

Make the most of ready-washed and trimmed leaves, scallions etc, and your salads will be ready in a matter of minutes. If preparing your own ingredients, make sure that you dry everything thoroughly, preferably in a salad spinner for ease and speed, and simply tear leaves with your hands.

For big mixed salads, use as large a bowl as possible so that you have ample room for tossing and mixing. A big shallow bowl is best as this makes it easier to ensure everyone gets a fair share of all the ingredients.

BASIC LEAVES	FRESH HERBS	VEGETABLES
butterhead lettuce	dill	cucumber, cut into julienne
romaine lettuce	parsley	bulb fennel, coarsely chopped
Belgian endive	thyme	bell peppers, seeded and snipped into thin strips
iceberg lettuce	chives	celery, trimmed and sliced
escarole	salad burnet	carrots, sliced or cut into julienne
lamb's lettuce (mâche)	tarragon	cabbage, shredded
curly endive	sweet cicely	Napa cabbage, sliced or shredded
red leaf lettuce	chervil	Snow peas, trimmed and blanched 1 or 2 minutes and then snipped into pieces
baby romaine lettuce	marjoram	cherry tomatoes
Treviso radicchio	mint	broccoli, separated into florets and blanched 2 or 3 minutes
curly lettuce	basil	sugar snap peas, trimmed and blanched 1 or 2 minutes and then snipped into pieces
Verona radicchio	summer savory	fine green trimmed and blanched 3 or 4 minutes and then snipped into short lengths
arugula	sage	baby corn, blanched 1 or 2 minutes and snipped into chunks
dandelion leaves	fennel	
watercress	coriander (cilantro)	leeks, rinsed, blanched 2 or 3 minutes, and sliced into short lengths
baby spinach	borage	
sorrel	hyssop	mushrooms, halved or thickly sliced
purslane	oregano	radishes, halved or sliced

BITS AND PIECES

walnuts, in halves or coarsely chopped

pistachios, lightly toasted and salted

melon, seeded and scooped into balls or chopped into cubes

oranges, peeled and thinly sliced

sunflower seeds, fried 2 or 3 minutes and lightly salted

Parmesan, grated or pared in thin flakes

sesame seeds, fried 1 or 2 minutes

strawberries, whole, halved, or quartered and sprinkled with black pepper

dill and fennel seeds, seasoned with salt and lemon juice

apples, cored and coarsely chopped or sliced

pine nuts, raw or sautéed in oil

hazelnuts, toasted or fried in butter and lightly salted

blue cheese, especially Roquefort, Stilton, or Gorgonzola, crumbled

avocados, peeled, seeded, and chopped and sprinkled with lemon or lime juice

croutons, fried in a little oil and butter in a pan smeared with garlic

poppy seeds, fried 1 or 2 minutes

black olives, pitted and whole or chopped

corn chips, crumbled

sliced almonds, toasted or fried in oil until golden and lightly salted

DRESSINGS

Basic Vinaigrette

Tomato and Tarragon Vinaigrette

Horseradish Mayonnaise

Lemon Vinaigrette

Garlic Vinaigrette

Mustard Mayonnaise

Soy and Honey Vinaigrette

Herb Vinaigrette

Balsamic Vinaigrette

Avocado and Sour Cream Vinaigrette

Walnut Oil Vinaigrette

Herb Mayonnaise

Basic Mayonnaise

Aïoli

Harissa and Black Olive Vinaigrette

Blue Cheese Mayonnaise

Orange Mayonnaise

Salsa Verde

Yogurt and Mint Mayonnaise

SALAD DRESSINGS

The simplest and quickest dressing for salads is a liberal dribbling of very good quality extra-virgin olive oil followed by a sprinkling of coarse sea salt and pepper. However, a wide range of interestingly flavored vinaigrettes are quite easily made. The salad should be tossed lightly to ensure that all the ingredients are coated with the dressing. Mayonnaise dressings are normally treated more like sauces and served separately or spooned over salads, rather than attempting to coat ingredients with them.

BASIC VINAIGRETTE

🕐   *under 5 minutes*

$\frac{1}{3}$ cup olive oil
1 tablespoon white wine vinegar
1 teaspoon Dijon-style mustard
salt and pepper

1   In a small bowl or cup, mix the oil and vinegar with the mustard until smooth.

2   Season to taste with pepper and just enough salt for the vinaigrette to stop tasting oily. Mix well again just before pouring over the salad.

Variations:
Lemon Vinaigrette: use lemon juice instead of vinegar.

Balsamic Vinaigrette: use balsamic vinegar.

Garlic Vinaigrette: mince 1 garlic clove into *Basic Vinaigrette.*

Herb Vinaigrette: use lemon juice and snip in some fresh parsley, chives, cilantro, basil, or fresh thyme.

Tomato and Tarragon Vinaigrette: whizz $\frac{1}{2}$ pound ripe tomatoes with a small pinch of sugar, 1 garlic clove, and $\frac{1}{2}$ teaspoon whole-grain mustard. Snip in some fresh tarragon and mix into a *Basic Vinaigrette* made with red wine vinegar.

Avocado and Sour Cream Vinaigrette: whizz flesh of 1 small avocado with 1 garlic clove and 2 tablespoons of sour cream; mix into *Lemon Vinaigrette.*

Soy and Honey Vinaigrette: use soy sauce instead of vinegar and stir in 1 tablespoon of honey.

Walnut Oil Vinaigrette: use equal parts walnut oil and sunflower oil.

Harissa and Black Olive Vinaigrette: whizz 1 tablespoon of harissa (Moroccan hot sauce) and 3 or 4 pitted black olives and mix this into the *Basic Vinaigrette.*

BASIC MAYONNAISE

🕐   *under 10 minutes*

Make sure all the ingredients are at room temperature to help the emulsion form readily. As the egg is not cooked it is essential that it comes from an impeccable source. Once made, store mayonnaise in the refrigerator.

1 egg
$\frac{1}{2}$ lemon
$\frac{3}{4}$ cup olive oil
$\frac{3}{4}$ cup sunflower oil
salt and pepper

1   Break the egg into the food processor. Add 1 tablespoon of juice from the lemon and one-quarter of the mixed oils.

2   Whizz briefly. With the machine still running, pour in the remaining oil in a steady stream and process until thick and smooth.

3   Season with salt and pepper and a little more lemon juice, if necessary.

Variations:

Mustard Mayonnaise: add 1 or 2 teaspoons of Dijon-style or whole-grain mustard to *Basic Mayonnaise.*

Blue Cheese Mayonnaise: whizz 3 ounces blue cheese with 3 tablespoons of crème fraîche or sour cream, 2 tablespoons of olive oil, and 1 tablespoon of lemon juice. Season with pepper.

Aïoli: whizz 3 garlic cloves with 1 egg yolk and then pour in the oils as above. Season to taste with salt, pepper, and lemon juice.

Orange Mayonnaise: use orange juice instead of lemon juice.

Yogurt and Mint Mayonnaise: add 2 tablespoons of thick plain yogurt to *Basic Mayonnaise* and snip in a few fresh mint leaves.

Herb Mayonnaise: snip some fresh herbs into *Basic Mayonnaise*, as for *Herb Vinaigrette.*

Salsa Verde: whizz about 1 cup flat-leaf parsley with 2 whole eggs, 4 garlic cloves, and 4 drained anchovy fillets; pour in the oils as above; season with pepper and lemon juice.

Horseradish Mayonnaise: flavor *Basic Mayonnaise* with 1 tablespoon creamed horseradish.

MAIN-COURSE SALADS

It is an easy matter to boost a simple salad into a satisfying main course. The addition of some cooked potatoes, cannellini beans, or chick peas will give substance and crunch, while nuts or chopped hard-cooked eggs can add protein.

For those for whom a main course must contain meat, try arranging some Strips (see pages 46–9) on a bed of lightly dressed mixed leaves. Alternatively shred some smoked fish or chicken or cold roast chicken, or roll slices of cold meats into cylinders and snip them into strips.

SHRIMP, ASPARAGUS, and LIMA BEAN SALAD

🕐　*under 15 minutes*

1 small lemon
14 ounces frozen lima beans
12–15 asparagus tips
1 garlic clove
¼ cup olive oil
3–4 scallions
½ pound shelled cooked shrimp
¼ pound prepared mixed salad leaves
salt and pepper
small bunch of fresh chervil

1　Squeeze the juice from the lemon.

2　Put the beans and the asparagus in a sauté pan, sprinkle with a little salt, and cover with boiling water. Simmer gently until just tender. Drain well.

3　Rub the rinsed-out and dried sauté pan with the halved garlic clove, add 1 tablespoon of the oil, and snip in the scallions. Sauté a minute or two and then add the shrimp with another 1 tablespoon of oil. Sauté 1 minute only.

4　Meanwhile, shred the salad leaves into a bowl and add 1 tablespoon of oil with half the lemon juice. Season well with salt and pepper. Toss well to ensure that all the leaves are coated.

5　Pile the shrimp mixture on top of the salad, arrange the asparagus tips and beans on top of that, and snip over the chervil. Season again lightly and dribble over the remaining oil and lemon juice.

SPICY AVOCADO and KIDNEY BEAN SALAD

🕐　*under 15 minutes*

½ pound broccoli florets or 1 large head of
　broccoli
½ pound snow peas
1 can (1-pound) red kidney beans
¼ pound prepared mixed salad leaves
whites of 3 fat scallions
1 large ripe avocado
¼ lemon
⅓ cup black olives
1 cup croutons
for the dressing:
1 teaspoon chili paste
¼ cup olive oil
2 tablespoons mayonnaise
1 tablespoon light cream
2–3 tablespoons orange juice
salt and pepper

1　Cut or shred the broccoli into tiny florets and put them in a saucepan. Sprinkle with a little salt and cover with boiling water. Simmer 2 minutes and then add the snow peas. Simmer 1 more minute and then drain well.

2　Meanwhile, drain the beans, shred the salad leaves into a large shallow bowl, and thinly slice the scallions. Halve, peel, and seed the avocado. Chop the flesh and squeeze lemon juice over it.

3　Combine the dressing ingredients well in a small bowl with salt and pepper to taste.

4　Pour a little of the dressing over the leaves and toss them well. Toss in the beans and sliced scallions with a little more of the dressing.

5　Add the olives, croutons, snow peas, and broccoli and toss with a little more of the dressing. Add the avocado and remaining dressing.

WATERCRESS, BEET, and HOT POTATO SALAD

🕐　*under 15 minutes*

1 pound baby new potatoes
2 cups watercress leaves
2 heads baby romaine lettuce
4 scallions
2 heads of Belgian endive
2 beets, cooked and peeled
for the dressing:
3 tablespoons Dijon-style mustard
⅓ cup olive oil
small bunch of parsley
small bunch of fresh chives
salt and pepper

1 Halve the potatoes, or cut them into quarters if large, and put them in a pan. Add some salt and cover with boiling water. Simmer until just tender, but still very firm. Drain well.

2 Meanwhile, shred the watercress and lettuce leaves into a salad bowl and snip over the scallions. Remove the hard core from the Belgian endive heads and snip them into the salad. Dice the beets into a small bowl.

3 Make the dressing: put the mustard into a bowl and gradually pour in the oil, stirring continuously, as if making mayonnaise. When the oil has all been incorporated, snip in the herbs and season to taste with salt and pepper.

4 When the potatoes are cooked, drain them well and add them to the salad. Pour over the dressing and sprinkle in the beets. Mix well to ensure that all the ingredients are coated in the dressing.

Spicy Avocado and Kidney Bean Salad

Variations:

1 Fry 3 or 4 slices of bacon and crumble them in with the potatoes. You can also deglaze the bacon fat with a little white wine vinegar and add that to the salad for extra flavor.

2 Hard-cook some eggs in the potato water and chop them into the salad. Use some of the egg yolk mashed in with the mustard to give extra body to the dressing.

6

DESSERTS

When there is no time to bake cakes, tarts, or soufflés, fruit is the salvation of the quick cook. Most ripe seasonal fruit is so full of natural flavor that very little help is needed to bring it out. We marinate fruit briefly in flavored alcohol, skewer exciting combinations of fruit on kebabs and broil them lightly, wrap them in packages and bake them for a few minutes, or purée with cream into fools.

Our other great ally is good vanilla ice cream which we recommend that you always keep in the freezer to serve with one of our five-minute sauces.

Various Fruit Kebabs (pages 84–5)

MARINATED FRUIT

Prepare the fruit before the meal and let it marinate, preferably in the refrigerator, stirring occasionally when you get the chance between courses. Serve with bowls of crème fraîche or thick plain yogurt, which can also be flavored with finely grated lemon, orange, or grapefruit zest. Garnish with a few tiny mint leaves or sprigs of lemon balm.

STRAWBERRIES in RASPBERRY VINEGAR with BLACK PEPPER

◖ *under 15 minutes*

If in a real hurry, don't bother to hull the strawberries, just wipe them with a damp cloth.

1 pound strawberries
coarsely ground black pepper
1 teaspoon confectioners' sugar
3 tablespoons raspberry vinegar

1   Hull and wash the strawberries. Pat them dry. Cut any large ones in half.

2   Place them in a serving bowl and sprinkle generously with coarsely ground black pepper. Sprinkle over the sugar and the vinegar. Mix carefully.

3   Chill at least 10 minutes.

CHERRIES IN EAU-DE-VIE

◖ *under 15 minutes*

1 pound ripe sweet cherries
3 tablespoons kirsch or brandy
1 tablespoon brown sugar

1   Remove the stems from the cherries, wash them, and pat them dry.

2   Put them in a serving bowl and sprinkle over the alcohol and the sugar.

3   Chill at least 10 minutes.

PEACHES in SPARKLING WHITE WINE

◖ *under 15 minutes*

Use yellow peaches which are ripe but not too soft to handle.

4 large ripe peaches
1 tablespoon cognac
$\frac{1}{2}$ bottle ($1\frac{1}{2}$ cups) well chilled dry or semi-sweet
   sparkling white wine

1   Wash the peaches and pat them dry. Cut them in half and remove the pits. Slice the halves again into quarters and then slice these again in two.

2   Put the peaches in bowls or pile them in tall glasses, add a dash of cognac to each, and pour in enough wine to cover.

3   Chill at least 10 minutes.

Variation:
Use the more delicately flavored white peaches, when available, but omit the cognac.

Clockwise from left: Strawberries in Raspberry Vinegar with Black Pepper, Cherries in Eau-de-vie, and Peaches in Sparkling White Wine

FRUIT KEBABS

Most firm fruit broils well in a matter of minutes. Cut pears, apples, and fresh pineapples in thick slices or chunks, quarter citrus fruits, halve apricots and plums, and leave strawberries and grapes whole. Make the kebabs before the meal and sprinkle any cut fruit with lemon juice to keep them from discoloring.

A wide variety of sweet butter sauces can be made to dress the kebabs by whizzing soft unsalted butter with any number of flavorings. Among the best are ginger, brown sugar, or honey, spirits, such as rum, gin, or whiskey, or liqueurs, such as Cointreau or Amaretto.

Always collect precious pan juices and spoon them over the kebabs.

PEAR, GRAPE, and CAPE GOOSEBERRY KEBABS

🕐   under 10 minutes

The cape gooseberry, also known as the "goldenberry", "chinese lantern fruit" or "physalis fruit", is enclosed in a delicate papery skin which should first be removed.

Orange and Lemon Butter (see page 51)
4 ripe but firm pears
4 cape gooseberries
about 12 large seedless black grapes
about 12 large seedless green grapes

1 Heat the broiler. Put the butter in a warm place to soften it.

2 Halve the pears and remove their cores. Halve the cape gooseberries.

3 Thread the fruit alternately on 4 wooden skewers, starting and finishing with a halved cape gooseberry.

4 Brush all the fruit with some of the softened butter and broil 1 minute on each side.

5 Serve with the remaining butter dotted or trickled over them.

FIG and GRAPEFRUIT KEBABS with MAPLE SYRUP BUTTER

🕐   under 10 minutes

The maple syrup butter goes well with many types of fruit, especially sharp ones.

4 fresh figs
2 small pink grapefruit
2 tablespoons sliced almonds
for the maple syrup butter:
4 tablespons unsalted butter, softened
2 tablespoons maple syrup

1 Heat the broiler.

2 Cut the figs in half lengthwise, or quarters if large. Peel the grapefruit and divide into sections.

3 Cut the butter into pieces and put in the food processor. Whizz with the maple syrup until smooth.

4 Arrange alternating pieces of different fruit on 8 small skewers and brush them with a little of the maple syrup butter.

5 Sprinkle them with some of the almonds. Mix the remaining almonds with the remaining butter and spread around the broiler pan.

6 Broil the kebabs 1 minute on each side, stirring the almonds in the pan from time to time so that they toast evenly.

7 Sprinkle the toasted almonds over the kebabs to serve.

STRAWBERRY and NECTARINE KEBABS with BRANDY BUTTER

🕐 *under 10 minutes*

½ lemon
2 ripe but firm nectarines
24 strawberries
for the brandy butter:
4 tablespoons unsalted butter, softened
1 tablespoon brown sugar
2 tablespoons brandy

1   Heat the broiler.

2   Squeeze the juice from the lemon. Cut the nectarines into halves, remove the pits, and cut them again into quarters. Brush them lightly with the lemon juice.

3   Cut the butter into pieces and put in the food processor. Add the sugar and brandy and whizz until smooth.

4   Thread alternating pieces of different fruit on 8 small skewers and brush them with a little of the brandy butter.

5   Broil the kebabs 1 minute on each side and serve dotted with any remaining brandy butter.

Variation:
Use plums and apricots.

● FRUIT GRATINS

Any number of fruits suit this treatment. Have the dish ready to go under the broiler as soon as the main course is over, but sprinkle on the sugar only at the last minute.

APRICOT GRATIN with CHOCOLATE SHAVINGS

🕐 *under 15 minutes*

8 ripe apricots
3 ounces semisweet chocolate
½ cup thick plain yogurt
3 tablespoons sugar

1   Heat the broiler.

2   Halve and pit the apricots. Pull a knife across the chocolate to curl it into thin strips.

3   Arrange the apricot halves in a gratin dish, hollows up. Spoon the yogurt over the top and sprinkle with the sugar.

4   Broil until the sugar caramelizes.

5   Dot the top with the chocolate shavings.

Variation:
For an even more adventurous dish, spoon a little marmalade over the apricots and sprinkle with a little orange liqueur.

MANGO and PINEAPPLE GRATIN with RUM

🕐 *under 15 minutes*

1 large ripe mango
1 large fresh pineapple
2 tablespoons rum
½ cup heavy cream
3 tablespoons brown sugar

1   Heat the broiler.

2   Peel the mango and slice the flesh. Peel, core, and slice the pineapple into chunks.

3   Arrange the fruit in a gratin dish or 4 flameproof ramekins and sprinkle over the rum.

4   Pour the cream over the top and sprinkle with the sugar.

5   Broil until the sugar caramelizes.

Variations:
1   A small pinch of freshly grated nutmeg and 1 or 2 tablespoons of lime juice will give an authentic Caribbean flavor.

2   Try replacing the cream with crème fraîche, or mascarpone or cream cheese.

● FRUIT PACKAGES

Wrapping mixtures of firm fruits in foil or baking parchment keeps in all their flavors and juices. They can be baked while the meal is in progress. Open the packages slightly as they are served to let the aromas waft up.

CHOCOLATE and BANANA PACKAGES

◐ *under 15 minutes*

4 ripe bananas
4 tablespoons unsalted butter
$\frac{1}{2}$ pound semisweet chocolate

1 Heat the oven to 425°F.

2 Cut out 4 squares of foil or paper large enough to wrap the bananas generously.

3 Peel the bananas and place them on the squares.

4 Put one-quarter of the butter on each banana and grate the chocolate over the fruit.

5 Wrap up the packages loosely, folding over edges to seal them well.

6 Bake 10 minutes.

RED FRUIT, and APPLE PACKAGES

◐ *under 10 minutes*

Use a mixed red fruit preserve with a high fruit content.

2 tablespoons unsalted butter
4 apples, such as Granny Smiths
1 cup red currants
2 tablespoons red fruit preserves
2 tablespoons kirsch

1 Heat the oven to 425°F.

2 Cut out 4 squares of foil or paper large enough to wrap the fruit generously and grease them with the butter.

3 Peel, halve, and core the apples. Cut the halves into thick slices and arrange them in 4 piles on the squares.

4 Take the stems off the red currants and divide them between the parcels. Spoon on the preserves and sprinkle over the liqueur.

5 Wrap up the packages loosely, folding over edges to seal them well.

6 Bake about 10 minutes.

PEAR and BLUE CHEESE PACKAGES

◐ *under 15 minutes*

This is a very good way of combining a fruit and cheese course.

4 ripe but firm pears, preferably Bartlett
1 whole graham cracker
2 tablespoons unsalted butter
6 ounces good blue cheese, such as Roquefort, Stilton, or Gorgonzola
6 tablespoons honeyed sweet white wine, such as Beaume-de-Venise

1 Heat the oven to 425°F.

2 Peel, halve, and core the pears. Cut the flesh into thick strips and cut out four large squares of foil or paper.

3 On each square pile a sliced pear and then crumble over one-quarter of the graham cracker. Dot with one-quarter of the butter and then crumble over the cheese, or cut it in small slices and dot these over the pears. Pour over one-quarter of the wine and then wrap up the packages loosely, folding over the edges to seal them well.

4 Bake 10 minutes.

Red Fruit, and Apple Packages

● FRUIT FOOLS

Use only really ripe soft fruit. Serve fruit fools accompanied by small cookies, such as amaretti or langues-de-chat (cats' tongues).

NECTARINE and ALMOND FOOL

🕐 *under 5 minutes*

2 tablespoons sliced almonds
1 pound ripe nectarines
3 tablespoons almond liqueur
$\frac{1}{4}$ cup heavy cream
about $\frac{1}{2}$ cup confectioners' sugar

1 Heat the broiler.

2 Scatter the almonds in the broiler pan and toast them lightly on both sides.

3 While they are toasting, pit and coarsely chop the nectarines.

4 Whizz the chopped nectarines in the food processor with the almond liqueur.

5 Add the cream and whizz again briefly.

6 Sweeten to taste with confectioners' sugar.

7 Sprinkle with the toasted almonds to serve.

GOOSEBERRY and ELDERFLOWER WINE FOOL

🕐 *under 5 minutes*

Use very ripe sweet gooseberries. The amount of honey may be reduced according to how sweet they are.

$1\frac{1}{2}$ pounds ripe gooseberries
3 tablespoons elderflower or other sweet white wine
about $\frac{1}{4}$ cup honey
$\frac{1}{4}$ cup heavy cream

1 Whizz the gooseberries in the food processor.

2 Press them through a strainer.

3 Return them to the food processor and whizz briefly with the wine and two-thirds of the honey.

4 Add the cream and whizz again briefly to mix.

5 If necessary, stir in more honey to sweeten to taste.

● *ICE CREAM SAUCES*

Probably the easiest means of providing a quick last course is simply to buy a good quality vanilla ice cream and serve it with a five-minute home-made sauce.

HOT WHITE CHOCOLATE SAUCE

🕐 *under 5 minutes*

2 tablespoons unsalted butter
3 ounces white chocolate
2 tablespoons heavy cream

1 Melt the butter with 2 tablespoons of water in a small saucepan over low heat.

2 Break in the chocolate and stir until it has all melted and the mixture is smooth.

3 Stir in the cream.

Variation:
Add 1 tablespoon of kirsch or other white brandy.

PEANUT BUTTER and JELLY SAUCE

🕐 *under 5 minutes*

2 tablespoons unsalted butter
¼ cup smooth peanut butter
¼ cup red fruit jelly or jam, preferably raspberry

1 Melt the butter in a small pan over low heat.

2 Add the peanut butter, mix well, and heat through.

3 Carefully mix in the fruit jelly or jam, but do not blend. It should be streaked through the sauce.

4 Heat through gently before serving.

RAISIN, HONEY, and GRAPPA SAUCE

🕐 *under 5 minutes*

3 tablespoons honey
2 tablespoons grappa or other white brandy
½ cup seedless raisins

1 Heat the honey with the grappa in a small pan.

2 Stir in the raisins and mix well to ensure that they are all coated.

Variation:
If you have the time, very gently simmer the raisins in the honey with half the liquor about 10 minutes. Stir in the remaining liquor to serve.

RED FRUIT SAUCE

🕐 *under 5 minutes*

6 tablespoons red fruit preserves
½ lemon
2 tablespoons raspberry or plum brandy

1 Heat the preserves in a small pan over low heat.

2 Finely grate the zest and squeeze the juice from the lemon.

3 Stir the lemon zest and juice and the brandy into the preserves.

4 Mix well.

7

MENU SUGGESTIONS

To help the reader make the most of the recipes in this book, we have set out a selection of menus for all occasions. They not only provide the necessary balance of ingredients, tastes, and textures, but also work well and efficiently in the kitchen.

Although a large number of our menus are conventional three-course meals, many are also built around the increasingly popular practice of making a meal out of two or three smaller dishes. This approach has the advantage of being highly flexible: Simple casual lunches or suppers can easily be transformed into formal dinners with the addition of one or two more dishes.

All our menus are strongly themed to help make selection easier, and for those in a really serious hurry our Ultra-quick section provides instant meals for all situations.

Carrots Vinaigrette (page 28)
Broiled steak with Blue Cheese Butter (page 59)
Twice-cooked Noodles with Baby Corn (page 68)
Nectarine and Almond Fool (page 88)

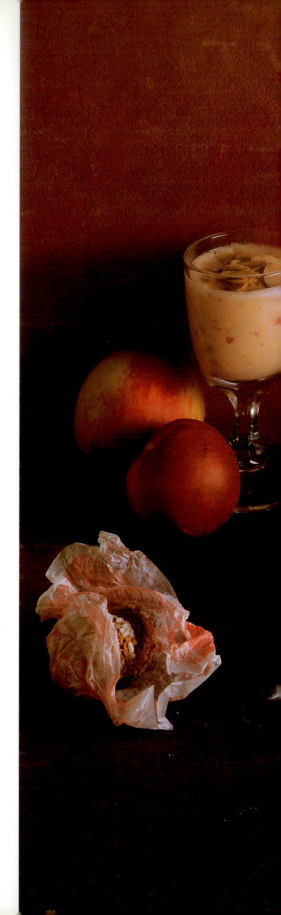

FAMILY and CASUAL MEALS

Quick Bolognese (*page 42*)
Salad of mixed leaves with Lemon Vinaigrette
(*page 76*)
Cheese and seasonal fruit

Quick Poule au Pot with Smoked Ham (*page 54*)
Baby New Potatoes with Fresh Herbs (*page 72*)
Ice cream with Red Fruit Sauce (*page 89*)

Pork Strips with Pizzaiola Sauce (*page 47*)
Tagliatelle with Poached Baby Vegetables (*page
42*)
Fig and Grapefruit Kebabs with Maple Syrup
Butter (*page 85*)

Herby Scrambled Eggs on Muffins (*page 36*)
Cannellini Bean, Garlic, and Curly Endive Soup
(*page 24*)
Yogurt with honey

Stir-fried Chicken, Oyster Mushrooms, and
Scallions (*page 55*)
Chinese no-cook noodles
Salad with Napa cabbage, snipped scallions, and
Soy and Honey Vinaigrette (*page 76*)
Fresh fruit

Cream of Mushroom Muffins (*page 34*)
Ham Steaks with Deviled Cumberland Sauce (*page
63*)
Buttered Baby Carrots with Vermouth (*page 70*)
Plum and Apricot Kebabs (*page 85*)

CHILDREN'S MEALS

Baby Tomato and Pesto Mini Pizzas (*page 32*)
Do-it-yourself salad (*pages 74-5*)
Chocolate and Banana Packages (*page 86*)

Quick Carbonara (*page 38*)
with added green peas and broccoli florets
Ice cream with Peanut Butter and Jelly Sauce
(*page 89*)

Potato Cakes with Bacon and Blue Cheese (*page
36*)
Green salad with a poached egg
Fresh fruit

Multicolored pasta shapes with Leek and Cheddar
Sauce (*page 41*)
Fruit kebabs with Maple Syrup Butter (*page 84*)

Beef strips with Blue Cheese Butter (*page 59*)
Spaghettini with Sautéed Zucchini Shreds (*page
69*)
Apricot Gratin with Chocolate Shavings (*page 85*)

ULTRA-QUICK

SPEEDY LIGHT LUNCH
Mixed leaf salad with watercress, lamb's lettuce,
and Stir-fried Scallions and Prosciutto Croûtes
(*page 36*)
Pear and Blue Cheese Packages (*page 86*)

ITALIAN MENU
Mozzarella, Anchovy, and Capers on Toast (*page 32*)
Broiled steak with Mustard Butter (*page 59*)
Mixed salad with Garlic Vinaigrette (*page 76*)
Blue Cheese and crackers
Mango and Pineapple Gratin with Rum (*page 85*)

QUICK SUMMER LUNCH
Mixed leaf salad with baby limas and Tuna fish,
Red Onion, and Olive Oil Sauce (*page 43*)
Strawberries in Raspberry Vinegar with Black
Pepper (*page 82*)

QUICK PARTY MENU
Gravlax and Crème fraîche on Rye Bread (*page
34*)
Noodles with Shrimp, Sugar Peas and Chili Oil
Sauce (*page 41*)
Salad of mixed leaves with chopped avocado,
snipped scallions, and Garlic Vinaigrette (*page 76*)
Peaches in Sparkling White Wine (*page 82*)

NO-COOK SUPPER
Cold Cream of Tomato Soup with Chervil (*page
20*)
Bresaola with Shaved Parmesan and Olive Oil
(*page 28*)
Salad of mixed leaves with kidney beans, crumbled
corn chips, and Harissa and Black Olive
Vinaigrette (*page 76*)
Cherries in Eau-de-vie (*page 82*) with thick plain
yogurt

COUCH-POTATO SNACK SUPPER
Pea and Smoked Ham soup (*page 22*) served with
Bruschetta with Ciabatta (*page 35*)

TRATTORIA SUPPER
Stir-fried Scallion and Prosciutto Croûtes (*page
36*)
Spaghetti with Salami, Parsley, and Olive Sauce
(*page 38*)
Mixed leaf salad with Balsamic Vinaigrette (*page
76*)
Ice cream with Raisin, Honey, and Grappa Sauce
(*page 89*)

VEGETARIAN

LUNCH ON THE RUN
Quick Soupe au Pistou (*page 22*) without the smoked ham
Green salad with Herb Vinaigrette (*page 76*)
Bread and cheese
Fresh fruit

QUICK AND EASY SUPPER
Baby Cauliflowers in Stilton Sauce (*page 30*)
Spicy Avocado and Kidney Bean Salad (*page 78*)
Peaches in Sparkling White Wine (*page 82*)

CASUAL ENTERTAINING
Grilled Mediterranean Vegetables (*page 73*)
Spaghettini with Crushed Nut Vinaigrette (*page 38*)
Cheese
Ice cream with Red Fruit Sauce (*page 89*)

SUMMER DINNER
Cold Avocado, Spinach, and Scallion Soup (*page 20*)
Tagliarini with Tomato and Fennel Sauce (*page 40*)
Green salad dressed with a little olive oil
Pear and Blue Cheese Packages (*page 86*)

COSY DINNER FOR FRIENDS
Cream of Mushroom Muffins (*page 34*)
Watercress, Beet, and Hot Potato Salad (*page 78*)
Mango and Pineapple Gratin with Rum (*page 85*)

ENTERTAINING

SUMMER'S EVE SUPPER
Cold Cream of Tomato Soup with Chervil (*page 20*)
Pan-fried Trout with Nut Sauce (*page 53*)
Peas with Lettuce and Scallions (*page 73*)
Peaches with Sparkling White Wine (*page 82*)

LIGHT SUPPER À LA MODE
Cold Fresh Herb Soup (*page 20*)
Jumbo Shrimp Sautéed with Ginger and Chili (*page 31*)
Salad of mixed leaves Stir-fried Scallions with Five-spice Powder (*page 72*)
Strawberries in Raspberry Vinegar with Black Pepper (*page 82*)

EASY BUT IMPRESSIVE
Bresaola with Shaved Parmesan and Olive Oil (*page 28*)
Salmon Steaks with a Light Salsa (*page 53*)
Baby New Potatoes with Fresh Herbs (*page 72*)
Green Beans with Anchovy Beurre Blanc Sauce (*page 69*)
Gooseberry and Elderflower Wine Fool (*page 88*)

MEATLESS MENUS
Guacamole on Walnut Bread (*page 34*)
Shrimp, Asparagus, and Lima Bean Salad (*page 78*)
Selection of cheeses
Strawberry and Nectarine Kebabs with Brandy Butter (*page 85*)

Papaya with Smoked Mackerel Mousse (*page 30*)
Tagliatelle with Wilted Spinach Leaves and Bacon (*page 41*)
Salad of mixed sharp leaves with pine nuts and Basic Vinaigrette (*page 76*)
Cheese

WINTER SUPPER
Grilled Radicchio with Goat Cheese (*page 28*)
Pork Chops with Apple and Calvados Sauce (*page 64*)
Stir-fried Leeks with Juniper Berries (*page 70*)
Ice cream with White Chocolate Sauce (*page 89*)

QUICK SUNDAY LUNCH
Rigatoni with Smoked Salmon, Sour Cream, and Chives (*page 40*)
Chicken Drumsticks with Salsa Verde (*page 55*)
Sautéed Zucchini Shreds (*page 69*)
Cheese and fresh fruit

DINNER À DEUX
Carrots Vinaigrette (*page 28*)
Broiled Steaks with Olive and Anchovy Butter (*page 58*)
Twice-cooked Noodles with Baby Corn (*page 68*)
Nectarine and Almond Fool (*page 88*)

INDEX